Cruising *with* Packky

SHRINIVAS & MUGDHA

INDIA · SINGAPORE · MALAYSIA

ISBN

Hardcase 979-8-89699-397-1
Paperback 979-8-89632-307-5

Contents

Foreword ... *5*

Acknowledgments ... *7*

01 Pack with Packky ... 9

02 Our Brush with the Titanic ... 21

03 Fly Away ... 27

04 Southampton ... 35

05 Embarkation Day ... 43

06 At Sea ... 51

07 Cork ... 59

08 Storm Agnes ... 69

09 Killybegs ... 77

10 Belfast ... 83

11 Dublin ... 91

12 Goodbye, Miss Starship ... 99

13 Amsterdam ... 109

14 London ... 129

15 Epilogue ... 143

Author's Bio ... *147*

Foreword

Hmmmm... you've read the blurb! Now should I have had a foreword by a famous author? I asked my publisher this, and he said it discourages readers from buying the book! That reminded me of a book where two famous authors had written 3 page forewords and that was about all that I managed to get through before giving up on it! So I'm having a go at it myself!

I had more thrills writing this book than actually travelling, that was my part of the fun!! Those of you who want to take the trip will get some inspiration for it! Those who've already done it in parts can reminisce about their experiences! And those who, like me, never want to leave their home can vicariously enjoy armchair travel! There, now I've given every single one of you a reason to buy and read my book! Go ahead then, why don't you!

Acknowledgments

I'm thankful to the Universe for having provided me endless entertainment in the guise of this book and I must acknowledge the particular parts that some entities have played in its genesis! I thank first and foremost Ganpati Bappa who saved me from Storm Agnes and arrived in Amsterdam to… check on us!

Next to be thanked, is the ankle ligament that tore and thrust inactivity upon me which in turn inspired me to write having just kissed The Blarney Stone, which awaits its mention here!

My friends and family, who read my initial efforts and laughed so much that I was emboldened enough to publish, are definitely more than a little responsible for this book seeing the light of the day! My dear Sister-in-law Anju merits a very special mention for her editing and her sheer enthusiasm and energy and encouragement!

And last… and first too, my long-suffering wife who is the butt of much of my humour and helped me rewrite it all in English and publish it, dealing with all the nitty gritty of designing the cover, graphics and interiors of the book, all of which are completely alien to me!!

But, above all, Art is nothing without appreciation and so, you dear reader whoever you are, Thank You!!

01

Pack with Packky

They say wisdom lies in knowing that we 'know' very little and that there's a great unknown beyond the scope of our known world. If so, I must be very wise indeed as most of the world is a big Potadi* of 'unknown' to me. And I'm never troubled by the slightest little wavelet of curiosity about them, as if these things did not, for all practical purposes, exist in the world (for after all isn't our world what we carry in our head). I wish I could put some of the things I do know in this Potadi too, but that's a whole other book! Well, among the many, many things that had never touched, even the very fringes of my mind, was this thing called a "CRUISE". Sure, I'd heard a stray comment here and there about how much fun they were, from a couple of friends but not such as raised the slightest longing in my mind to 'know' them.

Well, all that was just about to change. Just over three months ago, Packky pulled out of her Potadi called Google (basically the same one that I label 'the great unknown') this great big ship called NCL Star and floated it on the serene untroubled waters of my routine home life (love, love, love it) and raised great big tsunamis in its wake! Oh wait, I need to back up and tell you who Packky is. Imagine if you will, this woman who has such a longing to travel that her default setting is pack and unpack, whose motto is 'run and find out' and for whom the Scout motto 'be prepared' means packing everything she might conceivably need in as small a suitcase as I can persuade her to take (a losing battle might I needlessly add); and you'll have my wife of thirty five years and our life together might conceivably be titled "On The Road".

The last thirty years have been a veritable smorgasbord of travel to practically every province of India except the middle (Madhya Pradesh) and the North East (Not to worry guys we're coming very soo (probably this year once she reads this) several times to the USA, UK, France (winner of the favourite country contest), Austria, Greece, Finland (In -48°C), Iceland (much the same), Singapore, Tanzania, Italy, Malaysia, Switzerland, Indonesia (48°C). I guess the only reason we get to be at home occasionally is that we're both gainfully employed citizens 😉 😉. Her colleagues are always asking her how long she's visiting Mumbai for this time 😒 :(

Planning a domestic trip is a piece of cake for Packky, easy-peasy, but it's the planning of our international trips which brings a militant sparkle to her eye and transforms her into her 'Google Queen Avatar'. She collates a whole host of information, sets abuzz all the telephone and internet wires (does the internet have wires?), and perfectly puts in place every bit of the itinerary, including "unplanned" days 😉 😋.

This time around too NCl cruises from Asian, Mediterranean, Northern Europe, Alaska were examined inside out for the weather, and whether we'd be interested in the itinerary, the number of days (too many), the number of dollars (much of the same), departures, how and when to board, how much to tip and so on. There was exhaustive or exhausting(?) information about all the restaurants on board – the deck maps of every floor on the ship, words like 'for 'Ard', 'aft', 'port', 'starboard', which ocean view cabin was best placed for exiting for an excursion, and most importantly the exact location of the spa 😉 The plan is exhausting enough to make a believer out of me, as to how essential the spa is on these trips 😉. By the time we left for Southampton to board the cruise we had a WhatsApp group named, what else 'NCL Cruise', filled with coloured deck maps which were further printed and tacked to fridge doors and other vertical surfaces all through our home.

This was a new type of trip, where the mode of travel was a destination itself, so she chose the smallest land destination to circumnavigate, i.e. Ireland. Then there were the excursions on the Irish land itself: Cork, Dingle, Foynes, Galway, Killybegs, and the more familiar names – Belfast and Dublin.

A great deal of thought and buzzing of aforementioned internet wires went on about whether the excursions should be booked via our cruise line (expensive) or local guides (risky) who would pick us up at the quay. Packky was very busy with all this online running around and her loyal support staff (yours truly) only had to charge her laptops, provide credit card numbers, CVVs, OTPs, hold cellphones out of various windows to be in the best position to catch the aforementioned OTPs – at the best of times Vodafone makes this a net practice for fielding – and if all the online running around twisted the back be back-scratcher and masseur in chief.

These online searches bore fruit in the form of Paddywagon Tours, a Dublin-based company that would provide us excursions at Cork, Dublin, and Belfast at a considerable discount to NCL. One unplanned day was planned at Dingle, and the rest of the excursions in Foynes, Galway, and Killybegs were arranged with NCL itself.

Now, every single blessed time we've travelled we have had long discussions, aka arguments, on the same topics over and over again! They're some kind of bargaining that's an essential part of our journeys unfailingly for over thirty years! The first point of contention always is how many days we'll be travelling for this time. My own opinion is

I ought to be allowed to return home a dozen days or so after leaving it. Such a nice round number of days – why even bread and eggs come in dozens. Now Packky firmly refuses to count the two flights onward and return as trip days and besides these she contends for three weeks at least 😫 Knocked down in the first round of sparring, I rise up to declare that though I'd love a long holiday, I have only 10 days of leave left this year, to which she promptly goes online on our company app and points out that it gives lie to my statement . Why my leave days have to be common knowledge available on the internet I give you leave to imagine. Then, it's sandpaper time where 21-23 days are carefully filed down to 17-18 days, which relieved me and our tickets were at last booked from 22nd September to 12th of October.

The next point to hash out, of course, is how many bags of various sizes will be allowed to accompany us to our varied destinations. Packky is the domestic head for the grievances cell of all suitcases and backpacks! She adopts them and not content with giving them a home wishes to see them travel to various parts of our world 😟 and I say that just because the airline allows us 23 kgs each, there is no reason to lug about 46 kgs (not the least because you know who is going to do the lugging, right?). Unfailingly, what gets me is the threat to shop for clothes as the carry-on is simply not sufficient. Shopping on a cruise where the prices of everything are like those of coke and popcorn in a PVR cinema, is enough to send chills down my spine and I agree to seventeen days of heavy-lifting.

A month before we're due to travel, all the bags come off their shelf to roost on the floor. Their contents are bundled back on the shelf, and in general, the house looks like a war zone. This is generally the time when our dogs go into a permanent sulk, and one of them, Dash, has bitten her, accurately identifying the root cause of chaos.

Dogs are so intelligent and human, as Packky says. Now comes the watching of endless videos on weather-appropriate clothing for the destination, how to pack the maximum clothes into the minimum spaces, how to divide a bag into compartments using cubes, and such other hints provided helpfully by YouTube (the internet really has a lot to answer for) and then proceeds to do exactly what she's been doing all along 😧.

Next, our doorbell rings at least five times a day with Amma Jaan** (that's how much we love her) delivering various cubes, vacuum bags to pack clothes into the least possible spaces, collapsible water bottles, labels for suitcases, and other such travel essentials. Whenever these arrive, pulling the article out of Amazon's beautiful packaging is like pulling a needle out of a haystack, and I'm left wondering how many trees we're cutting down in the process 😧.

This time too, Packky improved Amma Jaan's bottom line, and in there was one item that surprised me, considering by now that nothing she does should surprise me. There was, among the various items, a package of magnetic hooks that, because the ship is made of iron (will it float?), can be stuck to the ceiling and walls of the stateroom to hold lighter items such as napkins, jhola bags, scarves, hats, etc., so that they are easily accessible. Well done, girl. All these "essentials" are packed, and the bags stashed away, and there's peace at home for a while.

The weekend before we travel, these bags come down again, and now there's the weighing-in process. This is, as you may imagine, a weighty affair. In the dark ages (Pre-Packky), I would weigh my bags by stepping on a weighing scale and then repeating the process carrying the bag; a simple subtraction and voilà, you have the bag weight. But Packky is too professional for these methods. She needs a special scale to weigh her bags. Once weighed, these are further stuffed with – Stuff, as she declares from experience that her 'special' scale reads a higher weight than the airline machine. And so, we were finally packed with three of her bags and a small carry-on for me 😁.

My own packing is simple – 5 quick dry Decathlon pants and I know, I know they're trousers, been told so multiple times by you-know-who that pants are unmentionables, but my Marathi English will stretch so far and no further. They're in colours like dark brown and charcoal grey to camouflage dirt and stains and guaranteed to dry in a few hours if I decide to handwash them. Along with my t-shirts, hankies, socks, and underwear is my favourite garment ever – my LUNGI! This versatile, peculiarly Indian garment has this advantage that since it's tied around the waist and free-floating below, it needn't be washed frequently. By now, it's quite clear to you, that laundry – or rather the avoiding of it while travelling – is my obsession. Wrapped in my lungi, t-shirts, and trousers are various microwavable MTR food packets – paneer palak, aloo palak, dal makhani, jeera rice, and lots and lots of Girnar ginger masala readymade tea packets. This last magical potion just needs hot water to transform it into my favourite morning cuppa. Despite all this, there is somehow inexplicably some room to spare in my bag which magically gets filled with female garments (really?)

Besides the checking in luggage, there are two backpacks and what passes for a handbag which we carry onto the flight. These are filled with chargers for the various bits of technology that Packky needs: her camera, iPad and Kindle, universal adaptor, multi-plug spike guard, binoculars, slippers for indoor use, books, medicines, and a set of clothes each in case our luggage arrives late or, God forbid, not at all! On a recent trip to Bali, Packky's luggage disembarked at Hanoi but was too slow to make the onward connection to Bali and got left behind. It was delivered at midnight to her, and she immediately made use of her insurance to claim Rs. 8000/- for luggage delayed beyond 8 hours. Of course, for the actual money to appear in her bank, I made about thirty five phone calls and sent as many emails to the TPA.

That's the only time we've benefited from the travel insurance that we diligently purchase every time we travel abroad. I shudder to think of paying a single medical bill anywhere other than home at the prohibitive exchange rates. Besides, visa forms usually mandate the purchase of medical insurance. Every single time we go through the process of figuring out their silver/gold/platinum plans with all the disasters that might conceivably happen (hospitalization, getting robbed, flight delays or crashes, loss of or delay of luggage, even residential fires while you're out of your home 😠) I'm tempted to cancel the trip and stay home. Since I don't win that one, I'm very glad to waste this money (platinum plan for us), of course, believing in some tiny hidden corner of my mind that it's a case of carrying an umbrella so that it won't rain.

So, back to our carry-on bags, where there's an important item – another bag, a pretty huge one that's folded over in quadruple and stuffed in a slim jacket. This is to accommodate shopping and clothes that mysteriously inflate after being worn and so require extra space, and then just as an expecting couple goes to the maternity ward as, well, a couple but returns a threesome, our bags will make their way home with this additional stuffed new companion 😂

Along with all the stuffing in her handbag (a Thanksgiving turkey is nothing to it), there's the very important foreign currency. Though we've joined the digital and plastic economy, we wouldn't be Indians if we didn't also carry along some currency in cash. The last few days are full of important-sounding market enquiries from Bakulbhai in Bandra to Mukulbhai in Borivali. There's a lot of (to my mind pointless) haggling over prices, but Packky's part Gujju heritage enjoys sounding market savvy. She has followed the rise and fall of currencies over the preceding months and is ready to buy at an opportune time. All this talk about prices happens over the phone and all thanks to Vi antics, she's practically hanging out of the window while I anxiously scan the compound for eavesdroppers to this money talk. This particular trip was pretty complex currency-wise. NCL cruise is American, and their staff would probably like to be tipped in dollars, Northern Ireland is part of the UK - I gained a working knowledge of Irish history on this trip – and the rest of Ireland makes do with the euro. Phew! Three currencies to handle might seem daunting to me, but Packky was all gung-ho! The more complex the numerical game, the happier she is.

Two days before our departure, the rates are finalised, and Mukulbhai dispatched to our home a nondescript little man, Pareshbhai, with the currency. You'd never guess to look at him that he was carrying anything more valuable than a SIM card in that shabby rexine bag he holds out with all the colourful notes that, to my eyes, look an awful lot like Monopoly money. I've earlier put all Packky's jewellery in the bank and withdrawn cash to pay him in return for these very false-looking notes, and until the first one is used on our trip, I am very uncertain if I've got anything real in return.

I hand over all my notes to him, bearing Gandhiji's smooth bald pate on their face and get Benjamin Franklin's luxuriant locks in return. As usually happens, the locks are more valuable, so I get a slim pile in return for my large bundle. Maia, my little Shih Tzu, finds me turning these notes over and over with such care that she comes around to sniff at them! Since my own sense of smell is not quite as acute, I have to believe the motto on these olive green notes: "In God We

Trust," and in my turn trust that I've received the world's favourite legal tender. Then I receive a few Hamiltons, Grant Jacksons, and Lincolns (at last a familiar face) and now it's the turn of the Queen of the UK and pretty much everything the British laid eyes on in the 16th and 17th centuries. The pounds come printed on pretty pink paper that actually feels nothing like paper and bears on its face the young queen, so beautiful that I'm sure it's perfumed paper that Maia is eagerly snuffling. If I were British, I too would refuse to exchange this beauty for the grey-yellow characterless euro notes that follow, which don't bear any piece of history or pride but just what appear to be grey clouds on a dirty yellowish background. Psst... pretty sure it's a map of the European Union! We have asked for a lot of different denominations because it's much easier to spend, but on my part also, a sneaking fear of spending those 200 euro notes as I see a large chunk of rupees disappearing every time I do that. Like when Paresh Bhai asks for a further Gpay amount and when I scan his QR code, I see several tens of thousands disappearing from our account. Maia and I then make a team foray to our cupboard to safely lock these precious notes in the jewellery locker. Of course, Packky when home from work has to count again (Her maiden name is Counto and boy, does she live up to it) while also adding to it three change purses with loads of change - quarters, dimes, cents, euro cents, shillings - collected on previous sorties.

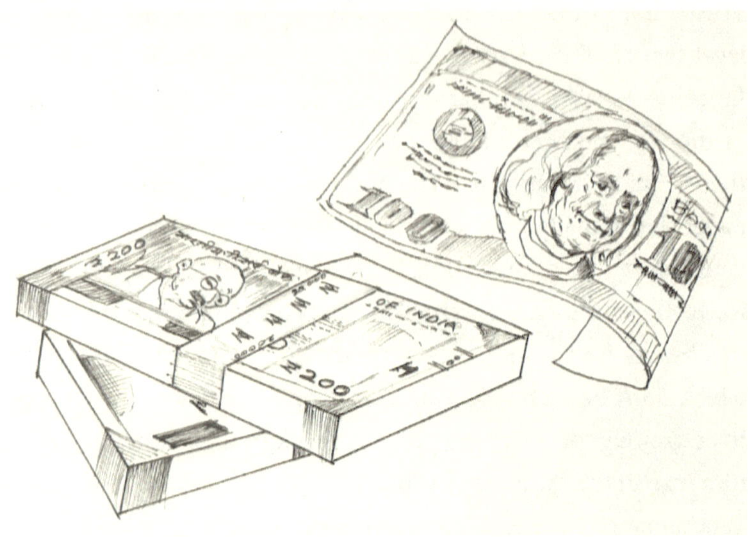

The next thing on the agenda is our data pack. This little thing is arguably the most important piece of luggage following the ticket and visa. Hunting out various locations on Google Maps, buying tickets to various boats, ferries, and museums, reading up instantly about anything of interest, looking for great restaurants, drinking holes, and cafes – the list of what Packky needs a data pack for is endless. I, on the other hand, need it so my patients can keep in touch with me and to speak to my kids back home and of course to contact her when I get lost in strange lands. And so having fortified this appendage called 'mobile', we are now done with all that we need before we fly!

And finally, the D-Day arrives when it's time to pick up our bags and depart for parts unknown! If this sounds like I'm going to fight a war, I'm embarrassed to confess it's not far off from what I feel. My preparations include a khaki uniform I got from Decathlon almost a decade ago that I pretty much wear only for long flights. The long-sleeved quick-dry shirt has multiple pockets with flaps that hold my passport, boarding pass, a copy of my ticket, and various documents that are considered necessary for humans to pass over borders they've drawn all over their maps. I envy the flamingos who make the trek from Siberia to Sewri with not a chit in their beaks. There's a hidden side pocket with a zip that holds credit cards and currency that I casually touch several times an hour just to make sure they haven't flown out somehow.

The trousers besides the normal pockets that hold kerchiefs and such have two flap pockets above the knee that hold earphones, sanitiser and a small vial of lotion! Thus, variously arrayed in clothes that serve as handbags I'm pretty much fortified and ready to travel. Besides this, there are two belts that I guard with my life which are strapped to my midriff. One goes inside my shirt and holds more currency and cards that's emergency money not to be spent but which nevertheless gets fingered every time I jerk awake in the flight or visit the loo, just, you know, to see if it's still there. Camouflaging this is a pouch that is the envy of all lady kangaroos, with six compartments that hold my travel essentials. The biggest one holds my cellphone and a diary I bought in Geeta Bhavan Rishikesh more than a decade ago. It has on every page a couple of shlokas from the Bhagavad-Gita and the remainder of the pages are filled variously with accounts of every trip, a few jottings from the same, and a few stray thoughts. As in everything the spiritual and the purely practical live comfortably together here as well. Other smaller compartments have a pack of rubber bands (to seal open bags of wafers and Milan supari, tie money bundles and some even to hold loose lidded boxes together), 20 packs of Milan supari (unbeknownst to Packky) and in the very last 3000 rupees that will finally waft me back from the airport to home on my return. Sitting there next to all the dollars, euros and pounds these little guys are going to spend the next twenty days (yup, I finally figured it out) feeling very down-mouthed at their poor valuation.

Packky, as usual, is in her onion-style disguise! Someone told her long back (usually it's advice from her sisters that she takes so much to heart) that to travel well, you must dress in layers! Well, she's well-layered with a sleeveless tee covered by a cotton shirt, then a jumper all topped off by her favourite large, well-pocketed denim jacket that has her passport, boarding pass, and cellphone. Packky usually avoids salons, but before a trip, the hands that stuffed the suitcases desperately need a manicure, and the curly grey locks that never ever see black or brown washes need to be arrayed in a rainbow of colours from purple, blue, green to pink. And thus, with our feathers fluffed and our dear son accommodatingly home to keep Maia company, we pick up our bags and descend the stairs to our waiting Uber after one last prayer to the Gods above to please waste our insurance.

---

* A large gunny sack, such as the one carried by rag pickers.

** Amazon

02

Our Brush with the Titanic

The extremely popular epic disaster film TITANIC starring Kate Winslet and Leonardo DiCaprio was responsible for many people learning of the actual real-life disaster the world over. Dubbed in many languages and grossing over 25 million, it gave the audience visuals that no one forgot in a hurry. The lavish sets, watching the massive ship sink slowly and crack down the middle into two, the people falling into the freezing Atlantic waters from great heights - all of it was absolutely unforgettable. The ship's string quartet playing their violins on the deck to calm people trying to board the lifeboats, the ship's chief architect and the captain calmly awaiting the last wave as an admission of their responsibility for the disaster, Jack (Leonardo) freezing to death in the Atlantic and his portrait of Rose (Kate Winslet) dressed only in the Heart of the Ocean (a large blue diamond necklace) - endless such vignettes are scorched into the viewer's mind.

The most famous scene of them all, however, indubitably remains "the pose." Jack persuading Rose to stand with him at the very top deck, nearabout the very top of the ship and stand arms spread to create a feeling of riding the waves and serendipitously seeing dolphins ride the wave at that exact moment - there are really no words for the feeling it engendered. There's just this that even today more than 25 years later, whether it be the rocks of Bandstand in Bandra or The Marine Lines, whether Manali or Yercaud, Kashmir or Kanyakumari, youngsters even today clamber up any precipice for the express purpose of re-enacting the pose. I have actually seen a Korean couple have themselves photographed in full wedding finery, bridal gown and all, in front of a famous Seljalandsfoss waterfall in Iceland during their pre-wedding shoot. Such is the fame and influence of the movie and that scene.

The actual sinking of the Titanic, on which this movie was based, happened more than a century ago. 10th April 1912 was the day that saw the launching of the Olympic-sized ship, The Titanic, on its maiden voyage on the Southampton-Cherbourg-Queenstown-New York route, being the then largest ship to cross the Atlantic. So large was it that even as it began to sink, it took the ocean two and a half hours to swallow it, with more than 1500 souls being lost in this tragic event. Over the years, many people have tried to solve its mysteries and all the whys and wherefores, including the recent disastrous implosion of the submersible Titan on an expedition to the ocean floor to view the debris.

Three months ago when we were first discussing the cruise, among the several tutorials I was given about the ship, the ports of call like Cork, Dingle, Foynes, Killybegs, what is a tender (small boat) I was getting bewildered by the unfamiliarity of it all. Would I remember all this even two months down the line? And suddenly—Kahani mein twist—Packky said, "You know, right, that Titanic took its last stop at Cork before it began its Atlantic crossing and then sank two days later." Just like that, the slow-starting movie suddenly became an eyeballs-glued-to-the-screen thriller. Really, there were passengers on the Titanic who had boarded at Cork who had walked the same ground we would be treading?

As soon as I heard the similarity of our cruise and the journey of Titanic, I began to encroach on her monopoly and began googling for information. Touted as "unsinkable", equipped with the most modern technology of the times, providing seven-star luxury rooms to the rich and the famous but also catering to the working-class population, she was the largest ship afloat at the time. She was supposed to cut the time of the crossing to New York by 24 hours if not more and was well advertised as such by White Lines, her owner. Furthermore, I had googled Cork and read that there's a Titanic Experience in Cobh (Port of Cork). Here they hand you a boarding pass of one of the 123 passengers who boarded Titanic at Cork, and then you experience in 4D (whatever that is) the actual sinking sensation of the ship. At the end of this realistic experience, you get to find out whether your passenger survived or sank with the ship. Since I never enjoy rides that send chills down my spine, I instantly decided not to visit it.

I also realised that we would be leaving from the same port that Titanic sailed away from, Southampton, and wished we'd booked some other departure. But somehow, I had to make my peace with it. Many of the crew of Titanic hailed from Southampton, and today there are plaques on the houses in remembrance of their tragic end. One of the differences in our journeys was that the ill-fated Titanic had taken in passengers at Cherbourg in France, which thankfully our ship would give the go-by. Another was that the Titanic, after leaving Queenstown (Cork), began its swift journey across the Atlantic, coming a cropper two days later, while ours would sail around Ireland in an attempt to circumnavigate it, just as if it were the Ganpati at Siddhatek where we go around an entire mountain as the idol is set into the mountainside.

Since we were now diverging from the route of the Titanic, I thought our further ports of call - Dingle, Foynes, Killybegs, Belfast, and Dublin - would be safe from its references. But imagine my surprise when I read that Belfast housed Harland and Wolff, which had built the Titanic, and furthermore had a museum shaped like the hull of the Titanic with a moat of water around it. I could actually see pictures of the lifeboats and life jackets of the survivors displayed there. Here I was, going on my very first cruise, having been told by the family astrologer in my horoscope that I would meet a watery end, and fates seemed to conspire to bring to my mind the most well-known maritime disaster of all time.

Deciding to investigate the similarities and differences in our two journeys, I read up about the decks, lifeboats, etc. Here I came across one of the reasons for the high number of lives lost. The Titanic was supposed to carry 48 lifeboats, but there were only 20 actually on it, not even enough for half the number of passengers on board. The reason for this being, a lighter ship would reach New York speedily, and a blind belief in its 'unsinkable' ness. Besides, even these few lifeboats were launched having been filled only to 60% capacity, leading to an increase in the casualties. The chief architect, Thomas Andrews Jr., and Captain Edward John Smith considered themselves responsible for the same and chose to redeem their honour by going down with their ship.

Having by now thoroughly frightened myself to no avail, I decided to give up the googling and consigned myself to floating on a sea of ignorance rather than diving nose-deep into the murky waters of Titanic's grave. Of course, the very first job on embarking the ship would be – COUNT THE LIFEBOATS!

03

Fly Away

Why is it that flights and trains are scheduled at 1.30 am or 00.45 am? We really need multiple calendar entries and notes to self, besides reminders from my assistant and Packky's staff, that a flight scheduled on 22nd September at 1.45 am actually meant an 8 pm or so exit from home on the 21st. I've had nightmares about realising too late that our flight has left without us! Besides, of course, the fear that traffic might snarl up, quite on purpose, to prevent us from reaching our check-in counters on time. So, of course, we end up reaching the airport a good four hours before the flight and have to contend with a long boring wait. Our various nieces and nephews are always amused as they barely make it in time to board, but our heartbeats can't take the marathon hammering this would induce! Of course, the airport has plenty of entertainment lined up for us, and now we start the steeplechase that has been arranged expressly for this purpose.

Though Packky checks-in online religiously (anything online is a religion with her), I don't see that it does us any good, as check-in luggage or not, we have to visit the counter for international flights. This is a very stressful moment for me! Whether our various bags will pass their weighing scale examinations, is the first point inducing palpitations. Owing to, once paying extra luggage charges at some horrendous rates, I've never ever let that happen again, but it doesn't stop me from worrying. Another stress point is whether various items have been correctly segregated into hand baggage and check-in – power banks in hand and large bottles of liquids in check-in! Somehow, we've managed not to mess up anything or at least not to confess to any misdemeanour, and with a large number of luggage claim tags attached to my boarding pass and one last look at our luggage trundled out of sight by the belt, we are passed on to the security checking!

To get into the security section for international flights at CSIA, there's no human looking at your boarding pass but a QR code gated barrier. Invariably, I have to rub my boarding pass beguilingly on two scanners before one gate grudgingly opens up, and I slither through and begin to disrobe in a bid to be declared fit to fly. Coat, shoes, belts, cell phones, chargers, Kindle – in short, anything metallic, electronic, and liquid must be separately placed on the tray to pass inspection. And once I am cleared, I have to put myself and my backpack together again as best I can, making sure I've picked up all my belongings before someone else does. Packky has, of course, done the same on the women's portion of the hall but having a great many more belongings and two bags, the unpacking has been accompanied by many mutterings about how the shenanigans of a few idiots in September 2001 changed flying for innocent good citizens like us. As usual, Packky's bright yellow Kipling does not make the grade and is passed down the FAIL chute, and she has to join a line of supplicants waiting to find the offending item in their bags. A patient security officer checks all the variety of compartments in her bag and is puzzled by a stiletto that doesn't seem to emerge even after emptying the purse. Finally, Packky helpfully pulls out a nail file that's burrowed itself into the lining, and he and I let out a sigh of relief and watch in disbelief as she manages to pack a huge tray of stuff back into her "purse" precisely as it had been before the disembowelment. Once past security, we face threatening immigration boards, that tell us to beware. If we're not polite enough to the immigration officer, we're going to be imprisoned. Of course, since we are unlikely to cause any trouble here, it's a shoo-in for us at this counter. However, I've watched a candidate or two go quietly (or not) crazy trying to argue about the sufficiency of their paperwork and the implacable immigration officers refusing to open the gate for them. The stuff of nightmares.

Speaking of nightmares, the airport helpfully provides a huge shopping arcade as punishment for daring to cross the immigration barrier. At one point in time, this wonderland for shopaholics had all the brands that weren't available in Aamchi Mumbai. Anyone who came back from a sojourn 'abroad' had a séance showing off or gifting (if you were one of the favoured) 'Phoren' goods. Now all the attraction is that being duty-free there's a slight discount in price, negligible in comparison to the prices of the goods themselves.

Already the sense of still being in my city has faded, and the recently concluded Ganesh festival with all its typical Mumbai flavour, the chanting of 'Atharvashirsha' invoking Him a thousand times has all been left behind on entering this peculiar airport world. There's a sameness to these shopping centres that makes them pretty soulless. No matter which city you may be in, the experience doesn't differ. There are pretty much the same brands with the same mind-numbing low temperature, bright lights, and colourful displays that have been calculated to part you from your money. Of course, the captive shopaholics have a field day here while I retire to the lounge, which is one of the free perks afforded by credit cards, where I can finally have a beer to soothe my frazzled nerves and tuck into a timely dinner. When to have this dinner is a problem for nutritionists to resolve. Should one eat at home to fortify oneself for airport shenanigans or eat in the lounge once you're free from these or eat, as some advise, in the flight, when it's closer to dinnertime at our destination? To be on the safe side, I eat all three dinners and am assured of enough blood glucose levels to snatch my twenty winks from an otherwise sleepless night.

And now, at last, we board the flight, stow our hand luggage in an overhead bin and settle down for the next 9 hours into an especially chosen and paid-for front seat in cattle class so my legs don't have to hold a 'cramped-asan' for the duration of the flight! Now while my legs are certainly given free rein, this wedged-in position of the rest of the body doesn't bode well for our comfort! Now is when I begin to wonder how many more millions would the business class cost us, having earlier watched as the prettiest air hostess plied them with champagne and hot towels and helped those who wanted to sleep instantly on boarding extend their seats into luxurious beds. I'm never tempted on land to buy one of these but put me in a cramped economy seat and the business class begins to beckon like a slice of heaven. I often wonder about the people occupying these, who's paying for it himself, whose office is providing them with the perk of easy travel so they're ready to drudge fresh off the flight. Oh, this lady seems like one of my aunts, maybe her kids are abroad and have sent her the ticket.

People generally fascinate Packky and me, and all our travels are populated with the stories we make up about people we observe on the trip. This seat has another great advantage-- I can people-watch all night as the washrooms are just ahead of my seat, and everyone in our section lines up in front of me at some point or another over the next few hours. The air hostess gets busy instructing all passengers in a mime peculiar to them on how to clip on their seat belts, open their window shades, stow away their tables, shut their cell phones, and have their seat backs upright. She holds a tube with an attached oxygen mask up in the air and dramatically lets it down to mimic O2 masks appearing in front of our noses in case of a fall of air pressure inside the cabin. I'm sure to be scared out of my skin if this were to actually happen. And of course, that one sentence that has spawned movies, novels, and endless lectures: "Put your own mask on before helping others." She next flaps her wings to indicate the exits while warning us that our nearest exit might be behind us. She also tells us, in case we have to jump into an ocean, which red tube to blow into to inflate our yellow life jacket. Not satisfied with merely scaring us, she proceeds to tell a very dodgy-looking guy next to the wing exits that he is in charge of opening the doors in cases of landing on water, but only after being expressly instructed to by the cabin crew. Knowing how most people can't follow push/pull instructions to open shop doors and invariably push where they should pull, I feel very aggrieved by this sloppy handover of responsibility.

The next order of business is food and beverage or rather the reverse. While our sly purser, Roger, is handing out coke and juices, I ask him for whisky. He and his trolley disappear, and I resign myself to wakefulness. But lo and behold! He turns up with two miniature red labels, and in an effort to thank him, I look past his swanky London accent at his name tag and realise that he's Rajiv, not Roger! Devoutly thankful for small mercies, I ponder on the trained flexibilities of pursers and especially air hostesses. Manoeuvring down narrow aisles in tight skirts with trolleys designed to exactly fill the aisles, crouching uncomfortably in a bid to hand over filled trays, brimming cups of drinks, bottles of water, and hot Styrofoam cups of coffee or tea, all with perfect manicures and not a hair out of place throughout the flight, takes a level of patience and skill quite beyond me. With the main business of the night over and done with, everyone in the plane settles down under their blankets to sleep or feign it in an effort to pass the night! I begin now to check out the various attachments and applications of my airline seat! There's the all-important (to pass the night) television screen that Packky magically makes appear out of a seat handle like some modern alchemist, its remote that shoots out on the pressing of a button like a sword expressly meant to enucleate my eye, hunting for the precise openings that the airline earphones jack will fit in, which portion of my back will actually be happy with the square pillow behind it (none), spreading the blanket on my knee – the entertainment takes up a good portion of the first hour. Then I settle down to watch a) an old favourite or b) as violent a K-drama as I can find.

And thus, having done my bit, of getting us closer to Heathrow, by making a good portion of the night pass, I watch the straggly stream of passengers queue up for their morning ablutions! There are different nationalities and personalities passing back and forth in various modes of dress ranging from sarees, trackpants to shorts. There are trailing shawls and humongous sweaters. There's even what looks to my untrained eyes like Pyjamas, but, Packky informs me, these are

Coord suits legitimately worn in public! Well, we live and we learn! Most are trying to stretch the kinks out of their system while waiting, with some actually going through a toe-touching asana routine in the legroom in front of my seat! I wake up from a short nap to find a clueless four waiting patiently before an unoccupied toilet, and I gently signal the first one to nudge the door open. This takes me back to my childhood days in a Girgaum Chawl! We had toilets built in the yard behind our houses, and they were labelled with our surnames - Ranade, Patwardhan, Ukidwe, Barve. The door was made of two long planks with just enough room in between them that squatting inside gave you a perfect view of who was coming towards you with the customary pail of water so that right before they knocked, you coughed loudly enough to stay their hands. The pail of water was necessary because though this loo had an ancient iron flush tank with a long, equally ancient, rusted iron chain pull, pull as I might through my childhood, no water ever emerged out of that flush! This one in the flight was as updated a cousin of that loo as you could get! Every time someone went in, it'd light up green with delight and go red with unoccupancy! The flush and vacuum system worked perfectly, and let us take a moment to thank our stars for that because there were about 500 of us who needed it through the night! There were lotions and so many different types of paper in there; I was quite bewildered by them! As with most Indians, I do believe that paper has no place in a loo at all, so to be faced by six varieties of them for hands and face and other such body parts is quite befuddling.

Breakfast is now served by the still cheerful Rajiv (how does he do it? Maybe Packky can take lessons) and I have a choice of Indian versus English breakfast! Knowing that this might be the last familiar meal in a long while, I opt for the upma while Packky, who has, when in Rome, stretched to "When in English airspace, eat as the English do" opts for the obvious. Her breakfast has a rolled-up omelette, baked beans, sausage, and the ubiquitous bun that appears in every plate of food, even accompanying my upma and chutney, sambhar. Breaking bread is compulsory in airline meals! We have opted for a peculiar arrangement of seats, Packky opting for a window seat while I opt for an aisle seat. The poor hapless creature between us is Chandrachud from Coimbatore, a student at King's College London. He is now in a bit of a dilemma, having eyed both our trays and being thoroughly undecided about what to eat. Once that is done away with, he is grilled by Packky, who is also playing peekaboo with the child in the bassinet, oblivious of the fact that her bawling has kept most of us, including her parents, from sleeping all night long.

In the midst of all this fun, the captain makes his appearance over the ether and announces that we're just a few miles from Heathrow, though still several thousand feet up in the air. He mentions that while the air outside is -30°C, Heathrow is a pleasant 18°C, and we would soon be circling down to land. The cabin crew were busy with their routine of straightening back stowaway trays, and then we finally swoop down upon London! Packky and Chandrachud were busy photographing the green county spread below us. When she got a particularly enticing photo of the winding course of the Thames, Chandrachud and she got busy airdropping it to his phone. Even on landing at Heathrow, we had a long wait to step onto British soil. Rajiv, the purser who occupied the crew seat directly facing us, assured us that we would make our connections for Southampton, as he also had a lot of passengers with onward international flights. We figured out during this chat that his residence was in Borivali, which is the suburb we stay at in Mumbai. He finally got the signal to announce that the passengers could retrieve their luggage from the overhead bins and disembark. All the cabin crew put on their headgear and coats, and—waving a friendly goodbye while exhorting us to fly British Airways again—finally allowed us onto the tarmac at Heathrow.

04

Southampton

One of the first indications that prove we've now become the "foreigners" is at Immigration in other countries! There was a separate line for those with a British passport and a long snaking line for "others" and joining the mandatory others labelled you instantly as a foreigner! This time, one of the ground staff was stacking cans of spring water at a curve in the line that we would repeatedly pass. This rather seemed like the peanut sellers at the traffic signal in Mumbai who magically appear when traffic snarls up and bode ill for a quick relief from the 'jam'! Packky was a little antsy at the possibility of missing our train connections to Southampton and having to waste money by rebooking! I, surprisingly, was very sanguine and full of confidence that the officials would clear the 'jam' in time! Besides, I was busy figuring out the workings of my water can that seemed to have more buttons than my A/C remote at home! Having picked it up on the principle of never refusing free water or a free visit to the washroom as abroad you often have to—shockingly—pay for both, I now found that it lacked the usual ring tab and had buttons and a push tab, that no matter what I did, would not open to release its cooling draught! About to fling it on the floor, in the hope that a nice jarring would do it some good, you-know-who came to my rescue and opened it with ease!

All this had kept me so occupied that I barely noticed that we were now at the head of the class and we were soon called to the counter together as we were a family! The young officer there asked us the usual questions of why we wanted to enter the UK (because the wife said so) and what we were going to do there. Packky, who can match a couple of dozen accents, having both understood and answered him, seemed to have convinced him that far from permanently staying here, we were just here to prop up the failing economy by converting a few rupees to pounds. He proceeded to stamp our passports with loud thuds (Why on earth!) as usual on some random page. Is there any particular order in which these guys are supposed to stamp these pages because a lot of them seem to randomly stamp any empty page they find! Not that I'm planning to use any information to point out to an immigration officer in a foreign land how he's made a mistake and argue with him about how he should be doing his job! Because immediately after stamping our passports, he presses an invisible button and lets us out unsupervised into his country which, for the sake of domestic peace, I would not jeopardise under any condition.

Now, we proceed to the baggage claim and exactly as eager young parents wait for their children to emerge from a kindergarten class, getting progressively more anxious as time passes and they don't spot their particular ward, all of the passengers on BA238 who travelled from Mumbai CSIA to London Heathrow eagerly wait around luggage belt 7 at Terminal 5. And just as the kids exit the school giggling and pushing each other, these bags that have made this long journey together are pally enough to jostle each other and tumble down the belt in delight at being out free after the confinement. I start to worry when a particularly large violet-coloured bag passes me thrice on the belt and none of my little ones have arrived! "Maybe they loaded them on another BA flight and the poor things are in Cairo", I say, to which she teases me, "This is London. There's always shopping." "Perish the thought," I mutter, and right on cue my darlings appear and we're on our way to catch our connection to Southampton.

As often happens on the extensive rail network in England, some portion of the tracks were under repair, a bus was being used to substitute the portion from Heathrow to Woking! There was a lot of talking to various airport officials, but Packky in record time located the machines and printed our tickets! Her chief joy on these journeys is to talk to various strangers, and mine is to give her a free rein as nothing bores me more, and thus we happily chugged along through Hounslow on to Woking! There we were to catch our train, and since there was some time before the connection, we popped into an M&S Eats and bought some sandwiches and a doughnut as insurance against hunger, though what with yesterday's multiple dinners, a sleepless night, and a long journey, our gastric juices were emulating Hamlet and repeatedly saying, "To eat or not to eat? that is the question!" We sat in the pleasant waiting room in Woking on the platform, and after some toing and froing, finally caught our train to Southampton.

Once there, Packky typed in 2 Georgian terrace, Portland Road as if she had been born and bred in Southampton, and we were deposited bag and baggage in front of our pied-à-terre at exactly 11.30 am. Now, Leo had allowed us to drop our luggage here even though it was way before our check-in time of 3 pm, and we placed our baggage in a vestibule just inside the front door. With a heavy heart, at least on my part, I may add, as I'd carefully watched the little ones since picking them up from school and didn't like to leave them unsupervised now. P on the other hand, has blithe trust in the world and Airbnb that has never yet been misplaced, I must admit.

And so we set out to explore Southampton. This first afternoon and early evening of exploring a new place is typically my favourite part of a trip. I might've forgotten most of the details of our many trips but the first day of each has remained etched in my mind in sharp relief against the blur of the days that follow. For example, on the first day of our very first trip, I remember the tall, curly-haired driver of our hop-on-hop-off bus, Phillipe, the Cinderella-like girl who drove our horse carriage, the dinner we had that night right down to the cherry tomatoes we forgot in the fridge of our hotel room in Vienna. My mind is like an eager sponge waiting to absorb all the new experiences served up to my heightened senses and all the differences in sights, sounds, and smells just serve to emphasise the departure from our daily lives. Southampton used to be a spa town and an important harbour, which latter function it still continues to serve. Though it's not a major tourist destination in itself, it receives more than 4 million tourists yearly due to the hundreds of cruise ships and transatlantic ships that dock here and begin their journey at its port. It was a cool, sunny, autumn day with a beautiful, blue, almost cloudless sky. The few fat clouds that scuttled across took on interesting shapes as they only do on a holiday. The High Street was quite busy with shoppers, which really, to a Mumbaikar, just means that it wasn't deserted but you could've happily twirled around, both hands laden with shopping bags, and not bumped into anyone. Compare that to a day out on Mumbai's Linking Road or Delhi's Chandni Chowk, an ordinary day out, mind you, which is a weaving in and out of crowds of people and the "busyness" of Southampton was muted. Even the absence of our street hawkers, rickshaws, large political hoardings, and loud honking of vehicles strikes one as does the silence! There seems to be a wider variety of people gathered here from Caucasians, Blacks, Asians, and an equal variety of costumes from the head-to-toe abaya to the short skirts and crop tops. There is a lot of hugging and kissing and eating and drinking on the street that's different from back home. I've always wondered why everyone seems to eat their breakfast, lunch and drink their morning and afternoon coffee on the go in the west. Indians, even while eating street food, seem to eat it standing near the bhelwala or vada pav wala rather than walking away with it. At the most, we ask him to parcel it, which he does in recycled newspaper, and then consume it at home, never on the go! I love drinking tea at the Tapris (small corner shops) dotted around India, but half the fun is standing there and watching the world go by. Indians everywhere seem to obey this unwritten rule as much as they flout every written one. All this eating and drinking peculiarly assaults my sense of smell and even back home, a whiff of coffee or cold cuts is enough to induce a moment of nostalgia or bring back a memory.

About 80 miles southwest of London, Southampton, though labelled a city, has the feel of a largish town. It has been inhabited since the Stone Age, and even today has city walls built in the 13th and 14th century. Because of its advantageous position as a port, it was repeatedly ransacked in medieval times, and the walls were built for its fortification. Many of its historical facts are set out on iron plaques on the footpath of the High Street, but since it was written in Olde English, it was not fully legible to us. As we strolled down High Street, checking out the Georgian Townhouses built by the rich who visited Southampton for its spa facilities in the latter half of the eighteenth century, we came across Southampton's famous Bargate. This is a broad, thick gate set into the city walls as an entry point from the docks. The walls are so thick that they hold a prison inside them, and this part of their history has been carefully preserved and restored by the English. This was also the site where our first photography session took place. Try as I might, I never seem to take a satisfactory photograph of my wife, and just as I was crouched in utkatasan trying to get the perfect angle, a passing girl tapped me on the shoulder and stretched her hand out for my cell phone, offering to take our picture. Since it's not a western trait to be friendly enough to offer to photograph strangers, I instantly knew that she was going to take off with my phone, but Packky's urging and glares had me very unwillingly hand it over to her. The result of it was a marvellous set of pictures of the two of us by the Bargate that were accidentally deleted when I did lose my cell phone two months later in Mumbai.

Right by Bargate was a small street stall by a Bangladeshi couple selling kebabs, naans, and biryanis. Just the sight of familiar food set off a longing to eat at the stall, but my stomach was still in an unresponsive coma, so reluctantly I left them behind to wander around the smaller streets leading to the docks. As always in these meanderings, we came across interesting stuff like the beautiful St. Michael's Church, the Duke of Wellington Pub, and the well-preserved ruins of the Holyrood church. It's the unexpected nooks and crannies of a city or town that make it memorable and the reason why we don't travel with too fixed an itinerary or with a travel company. This Holyrood church was destroyed in a blitzkrieg on 30th November 1940, along with several other churches, though just one street over, St. Michael's survived undisturbed. It is now a memorial to the brave Merchant Navy Seamen. Just a few doors away is a plaque bearing the name of one of the seamen who was a crew member of the Titanic that sailed from Southampton. Over 500 households in Southampton have been said to have lost at least one family member in that disaster!

After wandering through Southampton for a while, we sat down to a high tea at a side street café. I had a mind to check out the mouth of the River Itchen, of which I'd had a glimpse through the train as it pulled in, but there really wasn't time or energy for this. Besides, what could be more romantic than to leave something undone or unseen and have the hope of maybe someday coming back to see it! And so we slowly wandered back to our home for the night to wash our travel-stained garments in the washing machine helpfully provided by Leo and dry them on clothes hangers dotted around our room. Packky's task was to locate the dress she specifically wanted to wear on Embarkation Day, buried inside her suitcase. A glass of wine and a sandwich later, we were deep in slumber in the pleasant Green Room with a Victorian look in Leo's beautifully restored Georgian townhouse.

05

Embarkation Day

And at last, it was Embarkation Day! We were finally going to board the cruise that had stealthily caught hold of our imagination and brought us from Mumbai, India, to Southampton, UK. I'd prepared to don my travel uniform by running the washing machine yesterday, and Packky had packed a comfortable dress and jacket as her reading had told her to be prepared for a long day, because onboarding was usually time-consuming and tedious on NCL cruises. Wrapping up took no time at all in our Airbnb as we hadn't unpacked and, in fact, had left our suitcases downstairs and only carried our backpacks up to our room (think long creaky staircases). Though the port was very close and it was as fine an autumn day as you could get, the luggage mandated an Uber ride.

The driver, Arif, was Pakistani as it turned out! There is a special affinity to people from the subcontinent when we travel, and in fact, other than the namaj mark on his forehead, he reminded us of the theatre actor Rajit Kapur. Having broken the ice by telling him so, we were rewarded with a host of interesting information about Southampton, especially about the Maritime and Sailing exhibition currently being held, where Arif gleefully told us about the billions of pounds changing hands to buy and sell fancy yachts. In fact, we did have a look at the centre holding the exhibition as it was next door to the dock at which the ship NCL Star was docked!

Looming large above all the craft in the port, our humongous floating resort was about 13 stories or decks with large colourful stars and waves on her sides graphically portraying her name. From the 7th deck onwards, she was encircled by lifeboats all around, and my first surreptitious glance was to estimate whether they were sufficient in number for all the souls aboard. Having realised that the Titanic was inextricably linked with this particular voyage, I wished to be assured of the fact that we wouldn't in any respect partake of her fate.

There was a huge muddle of suitcases at the point where Arif dropped us, but the staff was efficiently sorting out the various procedures that guests needed to follow! We had, as I said, read that since it can take ages to get to our stateroom, we should plan our packing so that we carried just a few essentials like our swimsuits, documents, and cash in a small backpack and drop off the rest of the luggage at check-in! Special colour-coded tags denoting the position of our stateroom had to be affixed, and most of the guests were running helter-skelter to print them according to the format! Now, if there's one thing Packky is a stickler for, it's following instructions by authority, and so our tags had been printed back home in Borivali and affixed to all our bags the night before. In fact, they bore two tags beside this mandatory one - of our address back home and one of her nephews who lives in London and who we'd be visiting at some point on the trip. Talk about overkill.

That helped move us super-fast through the outer area to an inner, much quieter, organised room with the check-in counters! Our bags would have to undergo rigorous scanning for all the usual contraband and also for any food and drink items that were expressly banned on the cruise! Within five minutes, we were at the counter and our passports and receipts were scrutinised! Because we had Indian passports, the lady at the counter needed a little consultation with another colleague, and we realised that on the list at her desk where all guests were listed by country, we were the only two Indian passport holders. She came back and informed us that she would withhold our passports until the first port of call in Ireland where the immigration authority would stamp and hand them back to us! Now, this is one of the things that scares me half to death; here I am in a foreign land, and my one security blanket of touching my passport every now and then is suddenly snatched away from me, and instead I'm given a shiny new barcoded card which, besides the NCL name and logo, bears my name and stateroom number! For the next few days, this was to be our identity card, our keycard, our credit card, and until its safe return, apparently my passport too.

We had been prepared for hours of check-in time but magically were wafted in through a long gangway, whose glass gave us a view of our ship, up an enormous elevator to the now familiar card scanning gates! Unlike the airports, there were helpful staff here but presto just a whiff of my card and they opened wide to lure me in, and I was an NCL citizen bound for the sea! At every stage, we had been warned that the first thing to be done was to check out our emergency stations. We had been sent a video which described, among other awful things, procedures to follow if the ship caught fire, if it started sinking Titanic-style, if I fell overboard, and so on and so forth! Not content with scaring us into wishing we'd never spent our money so dangerously, we had to now report to the emergency station where we would gather in case of - right, an emergency! That done, we were left to our own devices, that is, I had been left to Packky's devices which are various and plentiful at the beginning of a trip. Our quick shoo-in through all the processes had been the result of commando-style preparation and training of this hapless recruit and was now further utilised to corner guest services and obtain various requisite bookings like those of restaurants and the spa on days at sea or other convenient times! To do this, required the agility to dodge various competitors for the same and accurate knowledge of, which counters were to be laid siege to! But who can trump the battle plan of The Bhartiya Nari from Mumbai!

And so triumphantly waving the desired bookings, we retired to Gatsby, which was the champagne bar to have our first drink on the ship if not at sea! While booking the cruise, Packky had been beguiled into getting a Free @ Sea package, which, like most freebies, must've cost an arm and a leg but delightfully allowed us to drink any wine, beer, gin, vodka, whisky to our hearts' content without counting the cost, which, as she well knows, saved me a lot of heartburn! It was practically an invitation for me to get pickled 😉.

Just as we'd settled into a dreamy state listening to the musicians at Gatsby's, we heard an announcement that our staterooms were now ready to welcome us to their bosom and, of course, sent us trailing there to take stock of our home for the next ten days! Our even-numbered room 5090 was an ocean-view stateroom, and all the odd-numbered ones were on the inside facing ours across the corridor. The corridor itself was carpeted with a bright red carpet that had tiny blue fish all swimming forward so that in case of disorientation (surprisingly frequent), all you had to do was check the little fish. There was, however, the odd larger fish that seemed to swim against the tide, and I have no idea what he was trying to say! This being the first day, there were a lot of crew members trying to help everyone, but the boards made it practically a sinecure.

One swipe of my card and we were in a narrow entryway with two closets facing one another! The one on the left had all the usual accessories in hangers and drawers, including the very necessary safe deposit box. The closet on the right turned out to be the washroom, neatly divided into a shower room, a water closet, and a washbasin area! It had a plentiful supply of snow-white towels in various sizes and also striped beach towels for the pool area, along with ten days' worth of toiletries worthy of five-star hotels! On any sojourn lasting more than 3-4 days, unpacking is the first order of our day, and this particular cabin/stateroom was going to house us for a little over ten days! Now my unpacking, as you can imagine, is quickly done! Clothes that are expressly bought because they're crease-free and easy to wash so travel is easier don't occupy much space or time, whether packing or the reverse, but the other half, of course, was neatly segregating night clothes, day clothes, dinner outfits, exercise clothes, swimsuits, and swim wraps, and a host of stuff that boggles my mind. Shoes to lounge in, pool shoes, dinner shoes, exercise ones, and walking ones followed to be neatly ranged on the bottom shelf of the cupboard, while mine were limited to flip-flops and the shoes I wore to travel in! Next, we attached the magnetic hooks to the walls, and I was inordinately pleased to see they worked very well, having had my doubts about these as about most things. They were endlessly useful to hang up items like hats and bags, but one item particularly troubled Packky. There was a long unfolding toilet bag filled with all the lotions and creams known only to womankind that refused to stay put and kept giving up the ghost every five seconds, until she remembered that the magnets are more powerful when hung perpendicular from the ceiling! And there it stayed put.

At this point, I was lovingly admonished to stay out of the way while she put away her accessories in the top drawer provided for the purpose! This seemed to consist of earrings, bracelets, chains, and necklaces of varying lengths and designs made of as many materials and metals known to man other than gold! Speaking of which, she locked all the various dollars, pounds, and euros into the safe deposit, barring some for distribution of largesse! I whispered, "Is the code the usual one for 'can't iron walls have ears too'?" And

I did so want to give the locker door a couple of tugs to check if it was securely shut, as is the hallmark of the Marathi Manoos, along with plastic pouches and bags used to wrap anything important like passports and money! But knowing the ridicule this would incite, I desisted, and we picked up our laminated cards and were off to explore our ship!

There was a Sail Away Party on the main deck with the swimming pool that we decided would be fun to watch while leaving the docks, so we wound our way upstairs to the 12th floor that had a little stage by the large Oasis poolside! Our ship was about 14 decks/storeys high with promenades from deck 7 onwards! These were also the storeys that had staterooms with balconies which were the premium economy section of the cruise, and the pièce de résistance was a garden villa on the thirteenth storey that was a huge suite of rooms with a garden sit-out! There was loud music and dancing by the poolside, and lots of people were in the pool already! People of all nationalities were gathered there, and it occurred to me that this was the first time I'd been part of a minority of just two Indians! Since I have two left feet, I didn't try the dance steps, but Packky did for a while before drifting to the hot tubs at two corners of the Promenade deck. One was luckily not in use, and we blissfully sank in and let the jets soothe our travel-weary selves. From high up here, we could see all the yachts gathered around the marina next door and realised that we were seeing the luxurious craft being traded at the exhibition next door! I made a beeline for the bar on the deck (they were scattered all over, literally) and brought over a glass of wine to enjoy while watching Southampton fade to a dot on the horizon!

Strangely, though, we didn't move at all from port. I realised that large container vehicles were unloading crates of provisions at the nether ends of the ship and correctly gauged that they were the reason for the delay. Hoping every one of the various chefs had accurately estimated (or better still, overestimated) and submitted their grocery lists so that I wouldn't go hungry at sea, we decided to exit the hot tub and dress for dinner and the show at Stardust Theatre. Not the least because the other hot tub now had a loudly yodelling guest who seemed to have taken free @ sea a little too seriously.

Waking up in the middle of the night, I glanced out of the porthole in our room and noticed that the lights of Southampton's port had disappeared. The vast ocean was all that filled my vision, and the sudden realisation that at last we were at sea gave me goosebumps!

06

At Sea

Mumbaikars have a limited view of the sky from their windows if they have one at all, and it takes one building next door redeveloped into a skyscraper for even this small bit of sky to be wiped out! Though we've widened our three-bedroom windows, there's just such a minuscule bit of sky seen there that leaves me hankering for more. It's the first thing I look for when I visit new houses - how much sky is apportioned to them? When the bright sunshine woke me up on this, our first lazy day on board the ship, the waters of the Irish Channel and the endless sky above it filled my view through the glass of our porthole! Utter Bliss! Wandering around Marine Drive in Mumbai as a child I kept glancing at the balconies of those sea-facing flats! I always expected to see people sipping their coffee and gazing out at the sea, but frankly, I never have! It never fails to amaze me! Now owning this window for ten days, I was like a child with a new toy. Making endless cups of tea, using the electric kettle, I squeezed onto the ledge and stared out. In fact, unlike the road and the crowds at Marine Drive, here there was nothing between the waves and me, and I could have sat there all day, but of course, fates, in the shape of Packky, had other plans.

Since of all the ten days we would have only three days entirely at sea on the ship without being offloaded for excursions, this first day was planned down to the T to thoroughly explore the ship and its amenities. The first port of call was the Yoga studio next to the gymnasium, which was a necessary prelude to delete all the sins of eating that we were going to commit all day! The trainer was Kamaal who lived up to his name with an amazingly immobile face and played some western music to accompany the light stretching routine he began. Rotating the wrists and ankles at his direction, I began to feel anew every one of the small bones of each hand and foot that we had been taught about in medicine. By the time he asked us to shake our hips like Shakira, I realized this was no Yoga class and lost all interest. Apparently for $20 a day, he would (possibly) teach us some actual Yogasanas, but since we've been practising these for some years now, we decided to find some other use for the $40 and practice by ourselves!

Next on our agenda was breakfast at Sheehan's, a bar and grill. Just as Mama Kane's and Kulkarni's hotel are named for the guy who owns them, this is apparently named after one of the former Presidents of the cruise line and serves as their central restaurant. It's open all 24 hours of the day and serves as a meeting place for those who feel peckish at 3 am. At the entrance, a smart young lady in a suit asked for our key cards and swiped them on her computer screen before politely leading us to a sea-view table laid with a snowy white tablecloth and napkins in which were wrapped our forks and knives and other implements necessary for demolishing our breakfast (at home in a hurry sometimes my fork comes wrapped in the very omelette that it's supposed to dissect).

Several unobtrusive stewards of various nationalities in their snowy white starched aprons were attending to the nearby tables, and one of them was politely urging coffee and orange juice on the breakfasters. They all bore name tags on their lapels, and our table soon saw Juan approaching and asking me if I would have the American or English breakfast. That cooked my goose properly, used as I am to pohe, thalipeeth, or upma options or toast and omelette being handed to me without any options at all. Followed, of course, by tea with ginger instead of orange juice and coffee. Just as we were finishing up our breakfast, the restaurant manager Ronny approached us. A jolly, talkative man, he was not just an Indian but also from Vakola in Mumbai, and he had the typical slang of "yes man, no man" that was so familiar to us. He had guessed that we were Indians but was equal parts surprised and delighted that we were actually Mumbaikars. We chatted for a while, and learning that we were doctors, he told us about his aged parents in Mumbai and their recent ailments with bits of consultation thrown in. Before he left, he urged us to have dinner at Aqua restaurant some night. "And I'll have the chef make you jeera rice and chicken curry" was like music to my ears!

One of the amenities included in the "free at sea" package that we had paid for (why was it called 'free' then?) was an internet pack of 150 minutes each! We'd never heard of a data pack measured by minutes instead of bytes! When we were kids, my sister Nanda and I would buy the 4 anna paper screw of peanuts, and mine would be gone in a jiffy, but she would halve each one and eat with relish, and her pack seemed to go on forever. We'd have to use similar strategies for our internet pack; it seemed, to make it last 10 days. So, we had, since the earlier day, carefully switched on the wifi connection, read and answered important messages, and immediately switched it off. Having at home a redundancy of network thanks to mobiles and unlimited wifi, we were unused to this economizing! Despite this extreme frugality, however, by this, the second morning, 100 minutes from P's phone and about 75 from mine had vanished! Equally bewildered and enraged at this, she dragged me off after our English Breakfast to the internet café so we could question this American cruise company, which rabbit hole our network was disappearing down!

Knowing that a lot of troubled people would attempt to breach their defences, the internet café had tucked itself away on a mezzanine floor with a discreet sign so as to be practically unlocatable. When we pushed the door to enter, we found another couple of co-passengers with similar woes. How people survived without electricity two hundred years ago is a question not more vital to us than how we were to survive ten days without wifi. The answer to all our questions appeared thankfully at 9 am on the dot, and since his English was like heavily accented German, it took much back and forth before he could get through to us that the wifi had to be switched on and off through an app, the app would release metered doses of wifi measured in minutes and would keep us informed about how many peanuts were left in the pack. Phew!! He not only downloaded the app for us but also grudgingly and after much checking of his screen and frowning at us finally returned about sixty minutes each of the wifi that had certainly not been 'used' by us! Being seriously techno challenged, it took me a couple of days to master these manoeuvres, and I used to carefully write all my messages and press send before ever I logged onto the net and quickly switch it off after sending the messages! One of the reasons is that one of my patients who had nausea and loose motions received only the antiemetic before the wifi failed, and I spent an hour thereafter praying to the wifi gods above (aka Satellites) and trying to send another message with the diarrhoea medication!

Having done this most important "job", we were free to wander around the ship, exploring it at will. Having seen the atrium of the ship while our glass lift passed it on the way to O'Sheehan's, we decided to start here. This beautiful four-storied space had huge panoramic windows separating it from the deck, and these had ledges where people spent time reading books, playing games such as cards, and Scrabble. On one end was a small stage where a talented musician was accompanying his own lovely baritone on a guitar. A few people sat in the chairs dotted around with their coffees and cocktails, politely clapping at the end of every song. On the other end were counters for customer care, accounts, excursion bookings, etc., where passengers were queued up to resolve their various queries ranging from the time of arrival at Cork to which excursion was available to book. The whole area was hung with sparkling chandeliers, and the stage was framed by two curving staircases!

Just such a red-carpeted staircase also descended in front of our favourite bar with live music, The Gatsby's! As we descended these, feeling like stars in an old Hindi film, we saw that almost all the tables were occupied. The tables had four armchairs each, and practically only two of these were occupied, bar a couple of larger groups. Luckily, Packky doesn't have a shy bone in her body, and with a polite "May I?" to which she received a smiling assent, we pulled up a couple of chairs and sat down to enjoy the live band. The ever-vigilant steward took our order, and with my first Jameson demolished and the second one cradled in my hand, I actually began enjoying the saxophone and trumpet and tapping along with the drums. I would've actually wanted just a small change here, and that is the 'chakna'. Apparently, all they had for snacks was a particularly hard, crispy corn, and I mentally asked them why, even after delaying us at Southampton, could they not load peanuts or chips onto the ship! Just a stray passing thought, however, as by now I was mellow enough to have their photographer take a couple of pictures on the staircase on our way out.

These photographs were part of our "Romance" package which also included two specialty dinners and thanks to the quick bookings done on embarkation, we had a reservation at Le Bistro, their reputed French restaurant tonight. It was for the early slot of 7 pm and our lunch or the corn at Gatsby's had contributed to my feeling stuffed even as we dressed for dinner at 6 pm. It's always a mystery to me why women wear black to a romantic dinner because I always thought of black as a colour used for protest! For whichever reason, however, twinning in black, we went down to the restaurant on the dot. Our appointment having been confirmed by a haughty young lady attired similarly in black, we were led to a table by the window by our steward Alec who smiled warmly at us and explained that he would be looking after us! Which he then proceeded to do by unfolding the starched napkins and laying them on us like bibs!

He then proceeded to uncork the wine and pour a thimbleful in each of our glasses and wait for our approval! My father used to have a thimbleful of Drakshasav whenever he had some gastric irritation and then burp loudly enough to be heard in every corner of our chawl, and now I was going to sample this wine! This is the moment of truth where it always crosses my mind - What would they do if I said I completely dislike the wine? It's similar to being frisked at the entrance of a mall - what in the world is that puny security guy going to do if I have a bomb or brandish a gun? There's no answering some questions – there's only swirling the wine and sniffing it, and then some more swirling inside the oral cavity, this time a quick swallow - and proffering of glasses for a heftier pour! Watching the sunbeams reflected on the waters of the Irish Channel reminded me of eating Bhel at the Girgaon Chowpatty watching the Arabian Sea sparkling under the Indian sun! But instead of the moustachioed bhaiya, I had before me, an ice bucket with a wine bottle, clinking wine glasses and… the Jack-in-the-box-like photographer who seemed to apparate out of thin air! Mellowed by the sun and the sea and the ambience, this time too, I allowed him to click a couple of pictures which threatened to turn into a full-blown session with awkward poses if I'd let him have his way! However, he disappeared into thin air as fast as the bread basket had appeared!

The warm, freshly baked bread in the bread basket was accompanied by a pat of butter, olive oil, and some herb dip! This is sometimes filling enough to make me wonder why we order any more, but of course, this dinner was already paid for. As Packky ordered unrecognisable dishes from the French menu, I spent the second glass of wine just having her decipher what we were going to eat:

Soupe Aux Quatre Champignons - Cream of mushroom soup

Cromesquis de Chèvre - Goat cheese croquettes

Carré d'agneau rôti aux saveurs marocaines - Roasted lamb in Moroccan spices

Coq au Vin - Chicken braised in red wine

Sole Grenobloise - Dover sole in lemon caper butter

Île Flottante - Floating island

Fraisier - Strawberry with cream

Alec brought soup and croquettes to our table all by himself. But when the mains were ready to be served, they were carried in with a flourish in procession of the maitre d', the chef, followed by Alec and two other stewards who carried the covered dishes raised in their right hand while their left was tucked away behind their back. The little procession came to a halt at our table and we were ceremoniously served. As they wished us "Bon Appétit", I felt really royal and for once did not mind the astronomical sum this must have cost. It was an evening to remember.

07

Cork

How to remember difficult words and nomenclatures, how in short to differentiate cerebrum from cerebellum and acetabulum from mediastinum formed the chief difficulty in the first year of being admitted to medical college. We invented a lot of tricks like visualisation, mnemonics, rhymes as memory aids. The amazing thing is these were effective enough that, forty years later also, I have fully and completely retained these tongue twisters and their associations. Now, these come in handy when I'm going to visit places whose names seem rather impossible to me. For example, our first port of call was going to be Cork, really Cork. Now isn't that the tapering brown stopper we use for wine bottles, only expensive ones too! But cork it was! So, visualise this - a large cork bobbing up and down on the channel between Ireland and the UK and Packky holding onto it for dear life because she was so looking forward to Cork! Now I might forget the entire cruise but this image of Cork is indelibly fixed in my mind!

At the end of nearly two days on the cruise after walking onto it at Southampton, we were eager as any sailor for the sight of land. At the break of dawn, a quick look out of our porthole showed a dark landmass, which, apart from a few twinkling lights at the harbour, appeared fast asleep. Half an hour later, we were anchoring at this harbour, and it was light enough to discern the board that said Port of Cork. There was the Irish Tricolour on one side of the board and on the other a flag that bore the legend - Port of Cork. A railway line ran close to the harbour with a tiny little station actually at the port itself to make it easier for cruise passengers to visit Cork! Beyond, still clothed in misty morning light, on a hillside were red tile roofs of a small hamlet with the distinctive church spire showing high above the other buildings.

You can just imagine our excitement to be on dry land after so long on the ship, so we were dressed and raring to go bright and early. Not the least because we were finally going to regain possession of our passports after the immigration officer had satisfied himself that we were fit to be let out onto Irish soil. This was to happen in the Aqua restaurant that was set up for this purpose, and there we repaired to await this final procedure. And we really had to wait long, as a queue formed behind us with everyone taking seats on the various tables that dotted the lounge. The guest services officer had assured us it would be done in ten to fifteen minutes, but this turned into half an hour and then an hour, and yet no one appeared to stamp our passports. Now seriously worried that I was going to miss our shore excursion, which had been booked independently with Paddywagon, I rather lost my temper and roundly expressed my displeasure. He sheepishly explained it was the immigration officer who was late, not the cruise officials. Next in line to us was a Korean girl who kept urging us to go upstairs to guest services to complain that we would miss our tour quite plainly, so we would forfeit our place in the queue. But Packky was too wily for her, and luckily for us, we stayed put, because in a few moments the immigration officer arrived and with a cursory look at our innocent faces stamped our passports, handed them to us, and we were free to go.

Or run… as the case stood for a while! We could see the yellow bus for the ship's own excursion; our green (supposedly) Paddywagon bus would be parked just outside the gates to the port. However, I didn't forget to confirm the time of return from the ship's officer while exiting the boat, lest I be left behind at the Port of Cork (always a very real worry for me). Walking alongside our cruise ship after disembarking, we were struck afresh by how really tall and large she was! We passed an Irish couple walking their two dogs, which is a sure shot ice breaker for Packky. "Oh! How sweet, which breed is this?" and such like followed, and they were equally friendly enough to say, "Oh, this is my elder one! And this is the younger." and share how the rambunctious elder fellow had become mellow and quiet after they adopted the second one! "Oh, that's the second child syndrome." I told them, entering the lists and surprising Packky.

Exiting the gates, we spotted the Irish green Paddywagon bus and the cheerful, round-faced driver checked Ramada (2) off his list of passengers. I wanted to sympathise with him because I have just as much trouble twisting my tongue around their Irish names. How, for example, do you pronounce Dun Laoghaire? Entering the bus, we were lucky to be seated immediately behind the driver where the panoramic windshield assured us of grand photos all around, except the back, of course. The mandatory first selfie of the day was quickly taken before the seat behind us was occupied, in case the lady behind us might object to us despite our palpably innocent looks! Though I actually prefer to get a few faces as a background for memories of faraway places! And as soon as all the passengers were ticked off our driver's list, we were off!

Cork is the second-largest city in Ireland, and its city centre is located peculiarly on an island formed by the River Lee dividing into two streams on the western edge and reuniting at the eastern edge. All this information was, of course, related by the driver of the day (Clark), who usually is like a Wiki page of the day. It rather reminded me of the Cité Island in Paris, which is similarly in the middle of the Seine! We passed the city of Cork in a jiffy and were soon in the rolling green countryside dotted with cows and other cattle that always look a tad bit healthier and more well-fed than the ones back home.

Dotting the landscape along with the cattle were tiny little tower-like castles which looked so toy-like that I was taken back to my childhood in a Mumbai chawl no. 3 Room no. 5, Angrewadi where we would build mud castles in the yard during Diwali and decorate them with flags made of scraps and toy soldiers! The interesting thing about these is (Clark the Wiki page) they were built at the behest of Henry the VI who, in an attempt to defend the Pale, promised a grant of 10 pounds to anyone who built a 20x16x40 feet castle on the edge of the Pale before 1439! That started a frenzy of castle building to rival us kids during Diwali and they on the last count numbered in tens of thousands, quite a few of which I sighted before reaching our first destination of the day, the Blarney Castle, and no, it isn't a ten-pounder!

This Blarney Castle visit had been in our conversation from the minute we decided to visit Ireland. I must be fit to climb the 150 steps up the castle was a constant refrain. "But we've been climbing the Lenyadri in our Ashtavinayak pilgrimage for years and anyway what does it matter if we don't climb it?" I countered. It appeared that the attraction was a famous stone called the Blarney Stone at the top of this castle which, if you manage to kiss, endows you with the gift of the gab. Imagine that! just some old stone and kissing it will endow you with eloquence – *why didn't the stone begin to talk?* I wonder. And if you ask my opinion, she doesn't at all require to develop her eloquence any further. If there's a stone you know of, that might reduce it a bit, by my entreaties, I'd go and smooch it in a jiffy.

Basically, I thought of it as a load of crap, but here I was en route to the famous rock! As we approached the castle, it dawned on me that there were extensive grounds and gardens surrounding the castle, as well as a river and lake! I also realised that the staircase was steep, narrow, and spiralled around the tower of the castle! Several enthusiastic stone kissers dropped out as they were unable to squeeze themselves past the opening! Clark had warned us that the staircase was one-way, slippery, and uneven! There was no turning back once we had our foot on the first pizza slice-shaped step, and onward we were to go! We couldn't decide to turn back halfway as the returning stairs were different and only accessible from the top. Having heard and heeded Clark's warning, some of our co-passengers chose to hang around the parking lot where there was a café and shop, while others made a beeline for the toilets and the gardens!

The intrepid two—armed with great shoes and the motto Jai Shivaji Jai Bhavani—caught hold of the rope as thick as a giant's wrist that gave purchase to the slippery foot and confidence to the climber and made our way up. It was early morning and so not a huge crowd, but there were people on the steps both above and below us, and everyone was careful not to spook or jostle each other even at such close quarters while at the same time holding on for dear life to purses, cameras, and suchlike! Through the arrow slits on the walls, I could see the people on the descending staircase and at some turns on the spiral, the beautiful river path that I immediately wanted to explore!

At last, we reached the roof and there, sitting by the stone, were two men! Just as on Chaturthi day at the Ganesh temple, two people give each devotee one moment in front of the Deity to fold his hands and bow his head before ushering him on, these two would seize the person attempting The Kiss, help him bend backwards over the precipice, and with a jerk of his/her neck, kiss the stone. Then they would help the Kisser up and spray sanitiser over the stone. Just one glimpse of this gave full-blown life to my fear of heights, and even though there was an iron grill preventing a fall, I decided not to attempt this foolhardiness. There was even a camera to record people in this most awkward position if they were willing to pay for it! Packky, just ahead of me, had already bent backwards over the precipice, and I noticed her glasses slip from her nose to her forehead. But she determinedly gave the stone a peck on the cheek, and one of the men helped her up! Now it was my turn, and before I knew it, I had been seized and bent over the precipice! I gave a mighty jerk of my neck but, alas, didn't feel my lips touch the stone! Since it was my first (and hopefully last) time kissing a rock, I smooched a flying kiss at it and was helped up by the guys! I realised that everyone was too apprehensive to have noticed my non-touch method with the Blarney Stone and happily made my way to the descending staircase! Down this way, there were a lot of rooms on display like the kitchens, salons, and bedrooms of the castle, but attracted by the outdoors, we made our way straight down and out of the castle door.

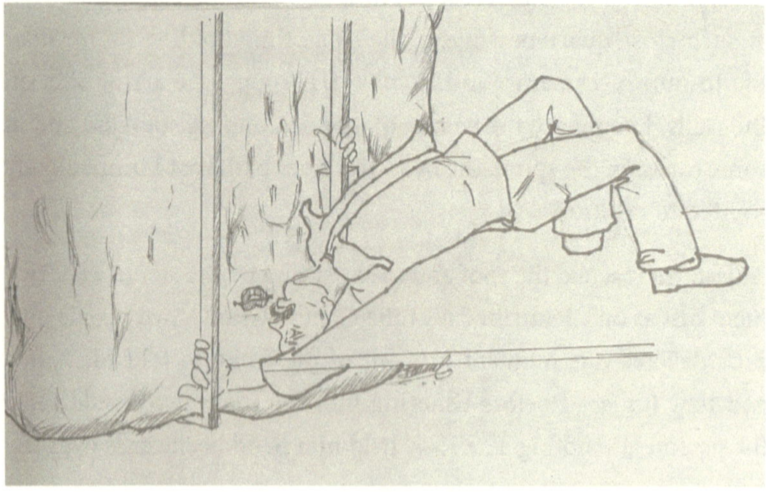

Just as we exited, the sound of lovely melodious bagpipes filled the air, and I realised that a local wearing a kilt was piping a merry tune on his bagpipes, which astonished me as I had previously thought this to be the sole province of the Scots! Followed by the lilting tune, we made our way down the river path and made a circuit of the extensive gardens until we reached the lake! This quiet walk, on which we were the only walkers, seemed almost meditative in contrast to the hurly-burly commercialism at the castle! Sweating in spite of the cool weather convinced me we were getting our day's exercise, and as we stopped to cool off by the lake, Packky tried to attract the attention of the three white swans swimming there by singing 'eka talyat hoti badke pille surekh'*! A futile exercise as I could have told her that world over, all that these greedy birds are attracted by is pieces of bread! Besides, they probably didn't understand the Marathi song being Irish, you know.

From Blarney Castle, we were to proceed to another extremely interesting place: The Old Jameson Distillery! Since the 18th century, this distillery has been almost single-handedly supplying the worldwide demand for Irish blended whiskey for almost 250 years! As of today, the 8 million cases of Jameson whisky sold in almost 130 countries around the world are produced in this distillery in Cork! In 1780, a lawyer, John Jameson, migrated from Scotland to Dublin and founded the first distillery, and his sons and grandsons ably carried forward his heritage for two centuries. When the American Prohibition era brought the Irish whiskey business into peril, several other distilleries joined hands with the Jameson Distillery, and the business grew to new heights through this cooperation. A really heartwarming story!

It was almost three in the afternoon when we arrived here, and there was another batch of tourists ahead of us soaking up the grains of knowledge that the guide was throwing their way and later just as eagerly the whisky too! Our guide had either inadvertently or otherwise left no time for lunch, so most of the people in our coach were a bit woozy and disgruntled. We'd managed to snatch a coffee and sandwich at the parking lot café and were not as cranky. A yellow-jacketed chirpy guy in his mid-forties introduced himself as Benjamin and shepherded us into the distillery with a merry "cheers"! The entire precincts of the Old Distillery make for a fascinating tour! For one, all of it has been as carefully preserved as all the old castles, caves, and other UNESCO heritage sites.

The old mill building we first entered, built in the early 1700s, was a military barrack before being bought and used as a mill from 1825! As we entered, Benjamin pointed out the struts being used to prop up and support the structure so that it wouldn't collapse during the tour! I wish people wouldn't point such things out as I immediately began to imagine such a disaster and sent up a prayer for intervention in case a strut should choose this day to give up. There were statues of farmers carrying in large sacks of barley as Benjamin explained how Jameson first experimented with barley mash to make whiskey to avoid the malt tax levied to import malt from Scotland. As a matter of course, those statues appeared in several Instagram selfies that day! I guess they're used to it by now.

Once our class at school was taken to a sugar factory, and there we saw actual farmers who had brought large tractors full of sugarcane to be sold there. How every last drop of juice is squeezed from this cane and then the juice boiled and boiled until crystallised, how the molasses are formed and filtered, and pure sugar is finally achieved formed the discourse that day. Somewhat similar to that, Ben told us about how the barley mash was fermented, and then swilled in the water of the stream flowing through the premises and then triple distilled in humongous copper stills. When I don't have to reproduce the knowledge for any test or examination, I take a lot of innocent pleasure in letting people prattle on about their various favourite topics! The massive copper still which was used for the distillation is now preserved in a glass room and is lovely and shiny enough to set off the selfie brigade rush! By now, I'd completely lost any focus on the process and was idly wondering what effect a hammer would have on the thick copper of the still while Packky, ever the interested student, was asking about the temperatures at which they boil the whiskey.

As we were guided out of the building into the compound, Ben showed us the really tall chimney that took the smoke from this process and let it loose high above the cityscape to prevent polluting the city. Right before us were enormous oak barrels or casks. Apparently, only new charred casks are legally allowed for Bourbon, so the once-used casks are sold to Irish and Scottish whiskey makers who have no such stipulation! Similarly, sherry casks are also reused by them. By now, my level of knowledge was demanding a practical demonstration by imbibing the product and allowing my palate to check that it was made to specification! This last piece of information did interest me; however, in so much that I saw how this large world of alcohol production cooperated and dealt with each other on multitudinous levels.

And now at last we were back where we started in their showroom cum whiskey tasting counter! Our tour included a free whiskey tasting coupon, and Packky, intoxicated by the day's activities, had generously handed me hers as well! All of us now made a beeline for the whiskey counters and then wandered around the aisles of the shopping centre! Anything and everything that could reasonably bear the name JAMESON was on sale there - bags, scarves, socks, caps, pins, handkerchiefs, glasses, and of course the actual whiskey bottles themselves, from the small 50ml mini bottles to large 4.5-litre ones. Though usually shunning shopping like the plague, having had more than my fair share of whiskey, I surprised the hell out of Packky by buying myself an Irish Green Jameson cap!

And now on our return journey, the formerly reserved and even cranky passengers were suddenly friendly and merry. Introductions were made, and the entire day discussed from the Blarney Stone to the Jameson Distillery until one by one we fell silent as tiredness from our day out overtook us. All the countryside and ten-pound castles passed in a blur of sleepiness, and Cork city just 8 miles away was soon reached. Although in the morning I'd thought I'd like to take a quick look around, the day had tired me out to the extent that I would've protested any attempt to delay my return. All I wanted to do was get home, that is my temporary home - Room no. 5090 on our ship! Just near the port of Cobh, the driver asked if anyone wanted to alight for a quick look at the Titanic Museum. I had long decided that the story was heartrending enough without seeing any proofs or memorabilia and had no hankering to even glance in its direction. So at last, we were dropped back home without further ado.

---

* A famous Marathi song based on the fable of "The Ugly Duckling"

08

Storm Agnes

After a busy time in Cork the previous day, we were looking forward to a good lie-in the next morning. Accordingly, I was happily in dreamland, having kissed the Blarney Stone, winning all debates with the formidable foe, and having her bow before me respectfully in the traditional style. Right at this moment of sweet victory, I felt her shaking me awake excitedly, saying, "Look, Agnes is here!" Agnes is our neighbour of many years back home in Borivali, and it puzzled me how she could suddenly appear on the cruise and why P was so excited about it anyway. "Arre, have a look at the screen, we are likely to run into Storm Agnes," made things clear, if not satisfactory.

We were anchored close to the landmass that was presumably Dingle, and the sea through our porthole looked angry and choppy. We had decided to take our time and wander around Dingle by ourselves and not on an excursion, so we went off to the Yoga studio. On our way back, we peeped into the Bliss Lounge to try and check out the process of taking a tender boat to shore, but puzzlingly, there was no one there. At the atrium, we finally heard an announcement that due to high waves and high-velocity winds, the small tender boats would not be approaching the ship, and so the scheduled port of Dingle could not be explored. Not very put out by this, we proceeded to our stateroom for "Breakfast in Bed," which was laughable as I had been shaken out of my bed a while ago.

At 8.30, there was a knock on the door, and two stewards stood there with what appeared to be a palace on wheels! This breakfast by room service was part of the 'Romance' package and as such was not only served with elegance but seemed to me to have food enough for our entire extended family and not just the two of us. Besides my scrambled eggs and her poached eggs on toast, there were croissants and scones, pastries and muffins, fruit of all kinds, and the crowning glory, a huge pyramid of chantilly cream studded with strawberries at all possible angles. Of course, all the other accompaniments like pats of butter, preserves, and two flasks of coffee made their mandatory appearance too. I doubted we'd have space in the room for all of this, let alone our stomachs, and wanted to offer help, but they smilingly declined and swiftly arranged everything on the tea table and writing desk. As we waded through this breakfast at leisure, reading our books with an eye on the sea outside, we suddenly saw a huge wave rise up and slap the porthole, which effectively killed the rest of my appetite.

Having seen this demonstration of what the storm was up to, I was actually thankful to hear an announcement from the captain that the ship would outrun the storm and take shelter near Scotland, effectively cancelling two more port outings after Dingle. Foynes and Galway. Apparently, the storm, though initially a small one common for the season, had undergone explosive "bombogenesis" and become a 'bomb cyclone'. My first thought was if it's storm season in the Atlantic, why in the world would you have a cruise ship merrily sitting in its way? One doesn't travel by ship from Bombay to Goa in the monsoons. Why, Mumbaikars barely manage to go to work!

For the cruise director Bianca, however, the irritated and restive guests and their entertainment posed a challenge of "cyclonic" proportions. The first point on their agenda was to assure everyone that this skipping of ports was being done entirely with a view to the safety of guests and crew alike and that they would be refunding a fee of $50 per port to all passengers besides refunding the excursion fees of anyone who had booked through them. Since we actually had booked the next few excursions with them, this meant that Storm Agnes would actually turn out profitable for me, if I lived to tell her tale! The cruise team then went to the trouble of publishing a new calendar of events for the day, filled with activities to entertain the guests in their enforced captivity and delivered it to every stateroom. P highlighted the activities she found interesting with a fluorescent marker brought expressly for this purpose, and we were off to a fun fitness class by Lucy.

Lucy was a Colombian with a heavy accented English that I found very difficult to follow. She began the class with Om chanting, which, since I had just recently chanted Atharvashirsha a thousand times during Ganesh Chaturthi with my family, rather galled me. But the class that followed demanded a level of activity that could hardly be "fun", and keeping up with all the women (yup, I was the only guy in that class) who, though in the senior range, sported bodies that would make twenty-year-olds weep, was pretty much exhausting. What with being on vacation and Agnes prancing outside, I was hardly up to strenuous aerobics. This was followed by some Christie-styled mystery quiz that Lucy put up on the board and read out to us. Having been schooled entirely in Marathi at Ram Mohan English School, I gave up before I began this activity, but P loves mysteries and solved it in a couple of tries.

Bored of hanging around the bliss lounge, we tried to access the open deck to check the weather conditions, only to find our access blocked due to the winds and slippery decks. Somehow, the waves splashing on the decks and the locked access doors made the storm seem far more real and close to home than before. We decided then to wander around the top decks of the ship and found that the swimming pool had been emptied and covered, and the topside grills and bars similarly closed down. We finally found ourselves outside the gym and Mandara Spa. The spa was making brisk business out of the storm (something like making money while the sun doesn't shine) and was enticing people with a free skin and eye check. Always wary of the spa and freebies, I declined, but Packky went to entertain herself, and as she's an eye surgeon herself, it probably amused her to check out what competition the cruise doctor could give her. Apparently, all he did was tell her she would have bags under her eyes if she did not use some of their products daily for the rest of her life.

We took up Ronnie on his offer of jeera rice and chicken curry at the Aqua dining room and replete with good Indian fare, I looked forward to a long afternoon nap. Just as I was falling asleep, Packky proposed that we attend a Bachata class at four which drew a groan from me. With a fervent prayer for someone to 'Bachao' me from this, I snatched my forty winks. All the cruise director's staff were Latin American and so of course, they were very limber and fantastic dancers. Bachata, which is derived from cha-cha and salsa, is an eight-step with a tap on the fourth and eighth beat, is what Tommy, the instructor, tried to tell me while performing seemingly impossible gymnastics with his hips along with the tap. If I could've imbibed half his skill and flexibility, I would be asking the printer for cards that said Dancer Ranade instead of Dr. Ranade.

This talented team of organisers had relegated Storm Agnes to the back of our minds, even if we had not forgotten it completely. Of course, the sheer luxuriousness of our surroundings allowed us to ignore the slight swaying of the floor beneath our feet. But that evening at the Stardust Theatre, the acrobatic jugglers who had been scheduled for a performance couldn't go onstage as the sway of the ship upset their balance. Instead, the dancer duo Katia and Zenia performed for us, and if we had thought Tommy to be a great dancer, he paled before these two. The audience, tired out by the relentless entertainment put on for them, whether bachata or mystery clues, wandered in with their drinks in hand and settled down to watch. The performance was greeted with generous applause, and after dinner, our first day in captivity was put to bed.

That night I woke with a start having been dreaming of our ship being caught in the storm. All my fears are most real and all-consuming in the dead of the night, and they threaten to take full possession of my mind. Usually at home, I visit the washroom without putting on the lights and keeping my eyes half-shut so that I should fall asleep instantly when back in bed. On the ship, the unfamiliarity confused me, and usually, we left the bathroom light on as a precaution against stubbing our toes. As I was going back to bed, my gaze fell on the porthole, and the movement of the waves seemed frightening in my half-asleep state. For the past few years, we had been having warnings of cyclones in Mumbai, which would begin over the Arabian Sea and be expected to cause havoc in Mumbai and its surrounding areas but would mysteriously veer off to have its landfall in Konkan or Goa or Gujarat and also usually to spend its fury mid-Ocean in the Arabian Sea. But this time it was us in the mid-ocean and a target for Storm Agnes! Somehow, I fell asleep, and the next morning after my bath, I said my Atharvashirsha, and then for good measure 21 of them: 'Tvamev pratyaksham tatvamasi, Tvamev kevalam kartasi' which means 'You are the navigator and the captain of my boat'. It immediately seemed to me that the boat was in calm waters!

That day had apparently started off with a commotion in the atrium as the TV channel showing the navigation map of the ship indicated we were anchored near Belfast, which meant we would have missed yet another stop of our cruise - Killybegs. The captain addressed the passengers on the PA system, assuring us that he would be able to dock at Killybegs on Friday and that the navigation map was faulty and would be disconnected and repaired. Packky was sure this was an eyewash and that we were sheltered between Belfast and Scotland and would simply backtrack towards Killybegs once the storm passed. Since I was feeling slightly seasick this morning, I was thankful to be in any place that would keep the ship steady. Luckily for me, the feeling passed after having toast and tea and never appeared again despite my fears. The captain also assured passengers of their safety and that he had sufficient lifeboats for everyone on board!

The highlight of our third day on board was a workshop on mobile cameras and their workings. Packky thought that I (or rather she) would benefit hugely from this as she's never happy with the photographs I click. Surprisingly, it was very interesting, and I realised that smartphones have outstripped their owners in terms of performance. Of course, as with anything free on the cruise, they were trying to sell lenses that could be clipped onto the mobile for wide-angle and zoom effects. A pack of three lenses was for 20 dollars, and everyone at the workshop seemed horrified at the price, so I was sure that meant it was 20,000 dollars. But as it happened, it was genuinely 20 dollars, and in a moment of euphoria, we bought them, which is why we have a lot of fisheye photographs of Killybegs.

Our ship had a lot of different restaurants offering various cuisines like Teppanyaki for Japanese Ginza for South Asian and La Cucina for Italian. Specifically included in our package was one of their two steakhouses, Cagney's, the other being a Brazilian Chiaroscuro. I was very suspicious of the word steakhouse, having grown up in Girgaon opposite Phadke Wadi Ganpati Mandir, watching people hand-feed the cows there and so unable to stomach the thought of beef. We had also read in a blog that vegetarians and vegans might want to steer clear of it as they would have limited choices. But an expedition there to peruse the menu reassured me that other items were freely available here and that night's dinner was taken care of. Surprisingly, we had good food and a good time at Cagney's, which may have been due to the excellent bottle of Merlot that accompanied the meal.

Halfway through the meal, the cruise director Bianca announced that we would be docking at Killybegs the next day and that Agnes had passed over and not done too much damage even in Ireland. There was a spontaneous cheer at this as all the guests were stir-crazy at having been confined to the ship for three days. Ahoy! Land at last! I could actually relate to the sailors of yore who would long to be on dry land after months at sea!

09

Killybegs

Our first sight of dry land after 72 hours of being ship-locked was exciting! We couldn't wait to set foot on the dock. That day, unfortunately, we were booked for an afternoon excursion with the ship! But we weren't going to wait until then, no siree! As soon as the morning excursion people disembarked, we ran down the gangplank eager to have a look at the little town of Killybegs!

This little port is known as a major fishing destination. Trawlers fish off its deep harbours, and the fish get shipped out to all parts of the world as far off as Japan and Africa. And so, here we were, just safe off of Storm Agnes, setting off on a brisk stroll around the little fishing town. It was bright and clear when we started out, but not more than five minutes into our walk, we were suddenly caught unawares by a shower! While I unfurled my umbrella, Packky ran to a nearby house to shelter under the eaves and don her raincoat and thus armoured venture forth again. Only to strip off the raincoat about another 5 minutes later as it became sweltering hot again. This happened thrice during the next half an hour, at which point I realised the truth of the maxim that Ireland shows you at least three seasons in an hour. Apart from a few stragglers, there was hardly anyone other than us. The population of the town is about 2000 in all, and every time we would shelter by the pretty porches of the large houses dotted around the area, it was brought home to me that I lived in a bustling metropolis with a population of 10 million where houses resemble matchboxes and the bustle is never-ending.

After this pleasant morning out of doors, we'd worked up quite an appetite for our lunch, which was perforce almost a brunch so we would be ready for our early afternoon excursion. Today we were going to try the lovely Garden Café that, while it had no garden, offered a smorgasbord of food in all its different varieties and that too in abundance. Soups, salads, pasta, pizzas, noodles, chicken sandwiches, roast chicken—familiar names ranged cheek by jowl with Turkey Chilli, Buttermilk pecans, White veal, Mushroom coconut Tilapia—of which I had absolutely no inkling. And then suddenly in one corner, I spied a counter with 'dal', rice, mixed veg curry with cauliflower and potatoes, chicken curry—Manna from heaven in fact! As I settled with my laden plate, I realised I was missing a familiar item but couldn't locate it on any counter. I was sure I'd seen it at breakfast time yesterday, so I asked one of the stewards for curds, but he shook his head! Disappointed, I settled down to eat without my "dahi". But Packky grinned and asked another steward to bring me plain yogurt and as a bonus even found some 'Poppadums' in a corner, which were in great demand. Now, if only I'd discovered this on my first day, I would have ended all meals, no matter the cuisine—Asian, Brazilian, English or French—at this garden café counter, polishing off my rice and 'dal' and 'dahi'!

That afternoon we were scheduled to join our ship's excursion to the cliffs of Sliabh Liag or Slieve League! Agnes had caused us to miss the opportunity of seeing the more famous Cliffs of Moher from Galway, so we were doubly eager to see these! Because Moher was a site for the shooting of a Harry Potter film due to its tremendously spread-out vistas and its accessibility, it is much more known and visited than its more rugged and spectacular cousin Slieve League, which actually stands sentinel to the Wild Atlantic Way towering at almost thrice the size of the Cliffs of Moher! However, accessibility is much less, and at the peak, there is what is known as a One Man's Path! Pretty self-explanatory! So, God plays favourites with cliffs just as with men, allotting more popularity and fame to one over the other! About 2 km before reaching the cliffs, our bus, which was diesel-powered, was stopped at a café called Ti Linn, and we had to proceed by smaller electric vehicles! The cliffs of Slieve League have the widest variety of alpine flowers in the county of Donegal, and these are sensitive to any changes in their fragile environment! Half the bus passengers went ahead in the smaller vehicle while we were treated to coffee and scones with clotted cream and strawberry jam! Surrounded on all sides by green fields dotted with sheep, the café had a heavenly location! Preferring to sit on the terrace, I soon realised the folly of it; my tepid English tea cooled fast, and to top that, I was distracted by all the paper napkins blown about by the stiff breeze! I finally gave up on my cold tea and helped the poor waitress running after the napkins, like boys run after paper kites during Makar Sankranti on the 15th of January! Happily, for me, she didn't tack on "Uncle" to her "Thank you," and before she could decide to address me as such, I escaped to the interior of the café! All my fellow passengers had already escaped to the warmer confines inside because a middle-aged Irish singer was singing old English songs, accompanying himself on his guitar, and the whole lot of them, including Packky, were carolling along!

Our fellow passengers returned laughing and chilled from their trip up to the tall cliffs, eager for their coffee and scones, and we made a beeline for the electric vehicles that would take us up.Being high-up on the peak, placed at a vantage position above the vast Atlantic, gave me a little thrill! Having just escaped the fury of the ocean in Storm Agnes and seen dry land safely, gave me a new appreciation for these massive sentinel cliffs whose ruggedness has engendered the name, The Wild Atlantic Way, for Ireland's western coastline! Ireland has a fascination for giants that shows up both in its folklore and in its geographical nomenclature. Directly below us was a set of rocks which legend has it, were the Giant's Chair and Table Everyone was busy admiring them while I had to confess to Packky that I couldn't for the life of me locate them. This kind of thing is always happening to me! At Tadoba, whole jeepfuls of people spotted a black panther perched on a tree in a thicket, while I saw only shadows, try as I might, to squint against the midday sun! Coincidentally, the panther was called 'Saaya', which means shadow! But Tadoba was within reach, and I could always go back and try to spot Saaya, not so this piece of rocky furniture! So, Packky began guiding my line of sight: "Look at that crooked tree. Spotted it? Now follow that line of sight out to sea, yes? Can you see that black rocky outcrop? Good. Now, look at the wave in front of that rock (???) Right beyond it, those two rocks make up the set." She was so triumphant at helping me locate it I didn't have the heart to disappoint her and, nodding my head enthusiastically, made my way down the One Man's Path!

The climb isn't dangerous but did give me some discomfort as I don't have a good head for heights! So I kept my head turned resolutely to the other edge of the path! There all along the descent I read several small boards that asked pet owners in no uncertain terms to pick up their pets' litter! Now this path was made of packed mud and any organic waste would simply become compost whereas the plastic bags used to pick up litter might definitely be around for the longest time! Pondering on the funny, complicated, and futile rules humans have made for themselves, I turned my back on Slieve League and headed for tomorrow's exciting destination – Belfast and the Giant's Causeway!!

10

Belfast

In the season of planning our travels, our home is inundated (me too), with a lot of homework on this subject! In the early days, there would be a lot of new books bought and strewn around the house, and their accompanying maps would be unfolded at the least excuse. Now, of course, the internet has saved us from so much paperwork but replaced it with eye fatigue due to the number of videos we watch! Two years ago, before our trip to East Africa, I had two months of zebras, giraffes, hippos, and rhinos parading around our TV in the evening and populating my dreams (nightmares?) at night! I was glad when we could go back to our usual Netflixing! This year, in the 'Irish' high season, I was told that 'Belfast' the movie was a must-watch, to improve my knowledge of Irish history, that is to say, to give me some inkling of it! When in medical college, in our third and final term, we were known as 'Exam Going' and this is when we would buckle down and cram as much stuff as we could! The inexorable bearing down of the travel season reminds me of this time, as when we are 'TourGoing', I am expected to gain a working knowledge of the history of the place and its people 😉.

Released in 2021, written and directed by Kenneth Branagh, Belfast is a movie that's an absolute must-watch, I was told! Branagh spent his childhood years in the neighbourhoods where conflicts erupted in the seventies, and his experiences are retold through the lens of Buddy, himself from a Protestant family but living on a street with

Catholic neighbours. How the clashes between the two factions impact their lives to the point that they migrate, as many Irish did during the Troubles, is told through the eyes of nine-year-old Buddy.

Having long been a resident in I.C. Colony, Borivali and having a lot of Christian neighbours, I was quite startled to realise that I had not much idea of their various factions and that the lines had been so drawn between them as to lead to riots in Belfast! When we were younger, I do vaguely recall reading about the Irish Republican Army, but that this situation was so bad as to lead a lot of Irish people to emigrate to the UK and the USA quite shocked me! I used to lump the entirety of the British Isles and their peoples into the label "English" or at the utmost the British without realising the hostilities that have been engendered amongst them by England's empire building! The very first time I realised this, was in Inverness, about 15 years ago, when our Scottish guide, Hugh, actually spat while talking about the white English lamb vs the black Scottish one!

Ever since watching Belfast, I was very keen to visit the neighbourhoods that had witnessed these scenes in reality! And here we were anchoring at the cruise harbour of Belfast, the capital of Northern Ireland, which until today, thanks to its majority of Protestant population, remains a part of the UK and uses the British pound as its legal tender!

Our driver for the day was the slim, very fair Martin who, at the very outset, boasted of having risen early and driven down from Dublin to reach us by 7.30 am. He was to drive back to his home in time for dinner once he deposited us back at the harbour! It was amusing to think that he would be in Dublin by dinnertime whilst our cruise ship would crawl the same distance and take all night long to reach the Irish capital.

As is usual, Martin combined both driving and being our guide in his skill set, and the moment he took his seat and began driving us away from the harbour, he evocatively laid before us his pride in his land and country and pretty much his hatred of the English for having long crushed Irish hopes under their heel! Listening to him tell of "Bloody Sunday", when a procession of unarmed Irish youth who were protesting peacefully were gunned down, brought our own outrage about the Jallianwala Bagh massacre vividly before our eyes! Martin's dearest hope was that a referendum in the near future would ensure Northern Ireland's uniting with the rest of the Irish and give them a sense of wholeness finally!

Listening to his passionate nationalism brought home to me, not for the first time, how many events and passions are giving shape to our world every second of which we are so ignorant or unknowing! This is pretty reciprocal as Martin has as little knowledge or interest in Borivali or, for that matter, India and its politics! All the while listening to Martin elucidating Irish history, my vision was enthralled by the greenery filling the panoramic windows of our bus and enjoying the smooth ride on the beautiful roads that allowed him to drive at a speed of 100 km/hr! You know how some days are just perfect; this was one of them. Before I knew it, we were at the Giant's Causeway an hour away from Belfast!

Located on the north shore of County Antrim in Northern Ireland and having been named a UNESCO heritage site, The Giant's Causeway is an extremely popular destination for visitors! All I could imagine was our homegrown Mahim Causeway, and just as Mahim Causeway joined erstwhile Salsette Island with Mahim and the rest of Mumbai city, this one is said to have at one time traversed the distance between Antrim's shore and that of Scotland! Consisting of about 40,000 interlocking basalt pillars that stand upright on the shore, this is a majestic site that floors you (especially if you haven't done any homework). On our way, Martin had explained to us that while archaeologists explain the formation of these as lava cooling in a volcanic fissure, the actual tale is explained by Gaelic mythology. As you can imagine, this appealed to me enormously as our own epics like the Purans, Mahabharat and Ramayan are what we earnestly believe in!

Well, according to this Gaelic legend, Finn McCool, the Irish giant, was once challenged to a fight by the roaring Scottish giant Benandonner from the opposite shore! Accepting the challenge, clever Finn built the causeway. However, as the Scottish giant approached the shore, Finn realised he was much bigger than him and he wiggled out of the fight by pretending to be Finn's infant son! Benandonner, who must have been more than a little dumb, ran away and destroyed the causeway behind him! This is why the tops of all the pillars form stepping stones that eventually tumble to sea level and then underwater! To corroborate, these stones are also found on the corresponding Scottish shores!

Having listened to this story, I was eager to see this wonder for myself! Being a World Heritage Site, our diesel buses had to stop a little away, and we would have to walk to the actual site. There was a path leading through a visitors' centre and another which took a little longer turn around it. The one leading through the centre cost 15 pounds each, so we took the cost-saving detour and immediately found ourselves on the shore where a fresh wind was almost blowing us backward! My bright green Jameson cap got blown off my pate, and several helpful tourists played catch with it before handing it back. I was eagerly scanning the shore for the stones and imagined the rocky shores to be part and parcel of it, while Packky was busy photographing birds (that looked like crows) and tiny flowers with her zoom lens!

And suddenly, as we neared the end of the path beside the cliff, I saw these majestic hexagonal reddish-brown columns packed tightly, in places as tall as Finn McCool and near the shore low enough to form seats to sit and watch the waves from. They formed a wall that was tall and wide and had a kind of opening in it. The tops of these pillars formed steps that gradually rose to a great height, and one could climb right to the top for a fantastic view. The arrangement and interlocking of these columns seemed to me to prove Martin's theory. How could these carefully shaped stones be an accidental occurrence? What do the archaeologists and UNESCO know? How could lava cool in such delightfully cool shapes!

Sitting high atop Finn's wall, I could see the two giants challenging each other, hear their roars, and as I touched the cool hexagonal tops, I assured them of my complete belief! Walking back, as in a dream, I felt I'd witnessed something marvellous and awe-inspiring!

Lunch today was in a typical Irish Pub on our way back from the causeway! Back home, the Irish Pub had been a topic of a tutorial in my homework! Apparently, unlike the bars in Aamchi Mumbai, it isn't where secret alcoholics stop for a daily fix! It is a place where whole families gather to socialise and down countless mugs of Guinness and cider! It's also famous for their folk musicians who belt out lively dancing tunes every evening. Unfortunately, we didn't experience much of this except for the Guinness! The pub was filled with most of us from Martin's bus, and the menu had been preselected by us, from the list Martin had passed around in the morning, in the interest of expediency! It had more than passed through my mind to wonder at the commissions Martin might be making at the pub!

Well, at the very least, if you enter an Irish Pub, having your fill of their delicious Guinness is a must, just as, when you visit Prakash Dugdha Mandir in Girgaon, you just have to taste their delicious Piyush! Along with swilling down the dark brew and wiping the foam off my moustache, I ate Clam chowder, which was a shellfish broth (thick soup) with lots of interesting ingredients. We ended the meal with a wonderful concoction of Sticky Toffee Pudding! Now, I had never had pudding before and wasn't even aware it was a dessert! But this particular one was absolutely delectable and made the highlight of a particularly satisfying meal!

The ride back to Belfast passed pleasantly in a hyperglycaemic (post-lunch) coma, where Gaelic giants chased each other merrily. Martin parked his bus at the Titanic Memorial garden, and we strolled around the Belfast city centre. Just then, it started to drizzle, and since we were close to the City Hall, we rushed in with our wet umbrellas for shelter. On the outside, it looked just like the BMC office, in the Fort area opposite CST in Mumbai! I didn't have very many expectations of it, especially with a heart full of the grandeur of the causeway! But the City Hall in Belfast was perfectly delightful.

Very well-maintained with a large, well-lit atrium, a grand staircase and gallery, an intricate stained-glass window; it said a lot about the city's pride in itself! There were exhibits of the history right up to modern times, and I quite wished we had more time to peruse these thoroughly. Even more astonishing, the public toilets rivalled those of the Taj Mahal hotel in Mumbai. I am a little finicky about touching toilet doors and usually choose a spot above the reach of most people (vagaries of the mind and the advantage of height), but here the door automatically swung open and shut by sensors! I experimented with them twice like a country hick. Another lovely feature was the café here that rivalled any posh café anywhere! Our government buildings have refreshment canteens that live up to this name, but this cheerful, airy, large tearoom had a plethora of choices. I ordered my usual, a large pot of tea, while Packky had an iced latte! For a chai bhakt like myself, watching someone have a cold beverage when it's cold and drizzling outside is unfathomable, but there, marriage will reconcile one to anything.

And so, we experienced a pleasant afternoon in Belfast, sitting by a window that gave out onto their garden, and watched the rain fall and the world go by! These are the moments, as you watch everyone hurrying to do their daily chores, that one is brought to a heightened awareness of being relaxed and on holiday. Total bliss! When we finally made our way out, we saw a makeshift stage erected on the lawns of the hall where a group of girls were performing a pop or rock song (don't know one from the other) and a threadbare crowd of friends and relatives standing in the light drizzle cheering them on. We strolled desultorily around the shopping district buying a few mandatory souvenirs for P's staff and my assistants until it was time to join Martin and our cruise gang again.

Martin had promised us a tour of the neighbourhoods where the proximity of the Protestants and Catholics had led to the beginning of The Troubles, and he drove us around these areas where the graffiti still declared people with definitive opinions. Currently, they declared solidarity with the Palestinians and many other overtly political posters. Martin's comments on these were that, even to this day, one wouldn't willingly be on the streets here after the fall of darkness and that there are gates between neighbourhoods still locked shut at 7 pm.

Driving back to the cruise harbour, Packky asked about the two tall orange cranes, that form a distinctive part of the Belfast cityscape, near the harbour. Apparently, they are the last remnants of the huge shipbuilding business carried out formerly in Belfast that even produced the famous or infamous Titanic. They are aptly named with a biblical reference as Samson and Goliath, and though they serve no function, the people of Belfast insisted that they should not be dismantled but remain as a visible symbol of their city.

Belfast truly unfurled all her magic upon us that day, and I felt I truly knew and loved it on this short acquaintance of a day's shore excursion!

11

Dublin

There are two types of ports for disembarking from the cruise, one which is deep enough for the cruise ship to anchor at, like Cork, for example, and one which is not deep and so has to be accessed by what the cruise ships call tenders (small boats that ferry you from ship to shore). In fact, Cork is one of the deepest natural harbours in the world, second only to Sydney. Imagine our surprise to learn that we would need tenders for Dublin. Now, the very first time we were to go by tender was at Dingle, and so, we hadn't planned any excursion there, as we wanted to take it easy and observe the process before committing to consign ourselves to a little boat in the middle of the Atlantic! However, Agnes put paid to all our plans there, and so we approached the tendering of the coupons for the tenders with all the preparation of a major board examination. We had a Paddywagon shore excursion booked for 7 am, and since the first tender only left at 6.30 am and took twenty minutes to reach the port, we had to be on it! Packky slept early that night after setting at least ten alarms, as the coupons for the tenders were to be distributed at 5.45 am in the Bliss lounge. The next morning, up at the crack of dawn or the tinkle of the alarm, she was dressed and off to the lounge at 5.30 am, thankfully, giving me time for a snooze. Plenty of other people had the same idea, and apparently there were a few minor skirmishes as people were scattered around tables in true American fashion and not queued up like the British. She emerged triumphant with an early tender, and we waited in the atrium for our turn to be called.

On a cruise as on flights, business class passengers get precedence to disembark (and everything else really) and the occupants of a huge garden villa, on the twelfth deck, were allowed to proceed before us! A hundred questions filled my mind as I approached the exit of the ship… *How small a boat was this tender... larger than a coracle I hope… will the steps leading down to it be wet and slippery as the warnings said... would I slip and fall into the mid-Atlantic?... Can the boat overturn and sink (overdose of Titanic)?... Would the waves induce me to be seasick? A distinct possibility given my genes… Should I have taken Avomine… but that would leave me too groggy to enjoy the excursion…* and suddenly I was on a broad iron staircase which I couldn't possibly have fallen off from, as it had proper guardrails, and where four large crew members stood on guard in case, I suppose, one of us decides to deliberately leap into the ocean. The boat itself was a large covered 100-seater with proper seats and no sense of imminent danger assailed me as I took a comfortable seat inside and waited until the last seat had been taken before being whisked off to Dun Laoghaire!

How much you enjoy a journey depends a lot on what your co-passengers are like, and though we had been travelling nominally with more than 1200 passengers, this was one of the few times that we were seated vis-a-vis people at such close quarters. To say that all our fellow seatmates were foreigners is superfluous, given that we were the foreigners on this cruise. An elderly quiet couple sat directly opposite us, and as is usual, Packky directly smiled and said hello to them, whereupon the husband immediately responded by saying hesitantly to me that he had been wanting to say that I reminded him hugely of Gandhi. Packky, of course, was intensely amused, and

I admitted that not just most of my male cousins but a quarter of the bald-pated males in my country shared the resemblance! The ice was now well and truly broken and we discussed our various occupations. He was an environmental scientist, retired but still taking up projects and doing some teaching, while she had retired as a biochemist. The talk naturally veered to environmental issues and how the huge ship, with its chandeliers sparkling all day and night and its tonnes of fuel use, was practically an assault on the environment and ended on Packky's remark, that Indians are still aspiring to the luxuries like ACs and cars and cruises, that Americans have enjoyed since the 1960s. So definitely the onus of cleaning house and reducing the carbon footprint was on the western countries rather than us! And as if on cue, the boat docked at Dun Laoghaire and spared us all a debate, though, I have to say, they took it in good spirit! Wishing each other a great day for our respective excursions, we sallied forth to check out Dublin and the countryside.

As usual, our Paddywagon bus was nowhere to be found, and we had to ask around a bit, before we found it close to the street, at the very entrance of the parking lot. We checked in with the driver and climbed on board, to find we were the only ones inside. It now dawned on us that we needn't have hurried, as the bus would not move from the lot until the last stragglers had arrived from the ship. An hour and a half and many tenders later, we were finally all loaded up and off to the countryside!

Usually given a choice of destinations, we invariably choose the countryside. So, before we actually had a look at Dublin, we were visiting Glendalough (Glen-Hollow between, Da-Two, Lough-Lakes) in the Wicklow mountains near Dublin. First inhabited by a monk, St. Kevin, who built a monastery here in the sixth century, Glendalough charmed us at first glance. The pretty rivulets running between the two lakes and then away into the valley, the wooden bridges crossing these, and the lakes themselves surrounded by the stunning green hills! England and Ireland have rain almost year-round, leading to this overflow of chlorophyll production that entices the eyes and makes it a sinecure for all visitors! The huge lakes were at two different levels, and as we munched on sandwiches and coffee at the café in the garden, we decided that we'd just take a leisurely stroll up to the lower lake and not hike right up to the upper one! It occurred to us, while we made our way up, that there was quite a crowd of people around, maybe not quite as much as our National Park at Borivli but even so a crowd. Watching teenagers get up to their antics and young couples with their kids in strollers, it dawned on us that it was a Sunday and Glendalough was a favourite picnic spot for Dubliners.

Wandering over the little wooden bridges over streams and through the wooded paths, we reached the lower lake. Here, we tarried at the banks awhile, and I idly watched a beautiful young mum try to encourage her cute toddler to feed the ducks. Packky, meanwhile, was deep in conversation with her dear sister, showing her the lake and its surroundings on a video call. As the camera turned round to face me, I pointed to the medieval monastery that could be seen in the distance through the woods. Though deserted and in ruins, it was a favourite spot for people to wander around and photograph.

Having had our fill of Glendalough, we turned our sights and the bus toward Dublin! Just after leaving the area, we reached a plateau where our driver, Eric, pointed out a hydroelectric power station with another lake. As he was very proud of it, all of us trooped out of the bus and dutifully photographed it, though truthfully, we wanted to be on our way to Dublin and lunch! And finally - Dublin - the Capital of the Republic of Ireland - pointing out some prominent buildings and monuments, Eric dropped us on O'Connell Street where his company office was located! This was the central street in Dublin and after warning us to be back at 5 pm, Eric let all his herd of tourists loose and went off for his lunch and probable snooze. Being lunchtime, there were a lot of people on the street, and we were surprised to see plenty of compatriots among them.

Meanwhile, we went up and down a couple of streets crossing O'Connell's, trying to scope out a good place for lunch! Considering that I was looking for a place that would not make me part with a thick wad of euros and she was looking for one with a lot of "Irish" atmosphere, it took us a fair bit of time. Finally, we agreed on one called The Grand Central Café, and found on entering that it was a delightful old pub, featuring furniture from the 60s era and serving good pub grub. Just at first, we were going to occupy their sidewalk tables and watch Dublin go by as we had our lunch, but since the very first five minutes turned up a hobo who wouldn't go by but insisted on telling us a tale in what sounded like Gaelic, we finally decided on choosing one in the cool inner recesses. There were two smart young waitresses clad in a black waistcoat and trousers who moved swiftly around taking orders and holding full plates aloft while serving their various allotted tables. Having ordered burgers and fries, we were free to people-watch, which is our favourite sport while waiting for our food.

Across the room on a table by the window was a couple that looked to be roughly our age. They seemed at home here, as if having a Sunday lunch at their favourite pub. However, we realised that they were having a rather serious discussion, almost sorrowful, and we wondered about the subject... Could they be discussing separation and divorce, or illness? Our food was served very quickly by the smiling girl, and as we demolished the burgers, the table next to ours was occupied by three ladies, again about our age. They had obviously been on a girls' shopping expedition and were chattering nineteen to the dozen! About ten minutes later, a young girl in her early twenties joined them and asked if she might borrow an empty chair from our table. They could all be seen excitedly exclaiming over her ring. This was wedding shopping for sure, sisters out shopping for a wedding in the family, we concluded!

Out on O'Connell Street after lunch, we made our way to his monument at the head of the street. There was the usual smattering of teenagers on the steps of its pedestal while O'Connell himself stands at the very top! There are many figures representing different elements of Irish society, including Ireland herself, with shackles cast off. This is because O'Connell is known as The Liberator of Ireland for successfully campaigning for the right of Irish Catholics to become members of Parliament. There are also four winged maidens representing his qualities of Patriotism, Eloquence, Courage, and Fidelity! And right above it all, statue-like himself, perched on O'Connell's head, was the seagull, that Eric, our driver, had promised us would always be there. His pose reminded me of nothing more or less than the small boys who climb to the apex of the human pyramid at Dahi Handi Time and break the handi!

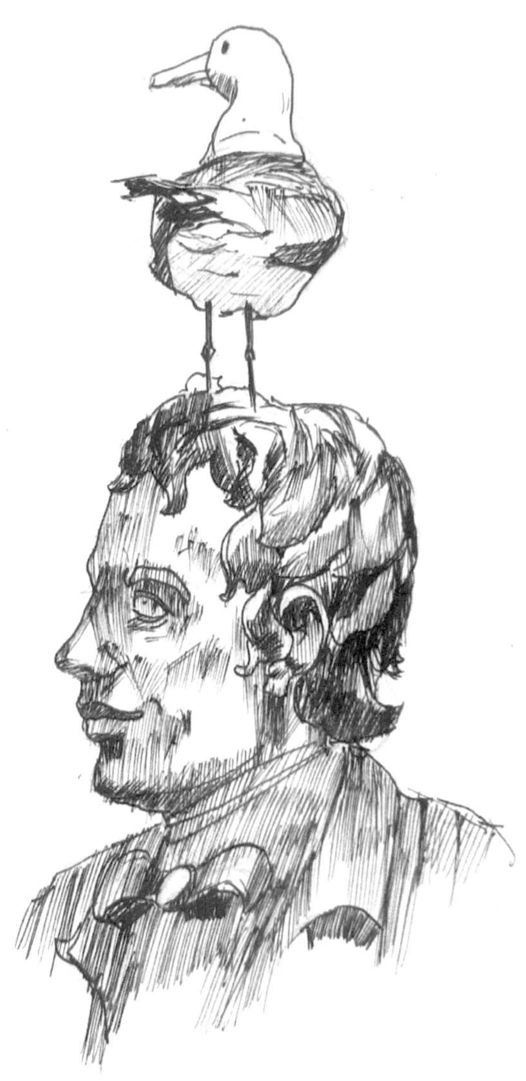

Strolling beyond the monument, we came to a bridge over the river Liffey, which was quite lovely and had the prettiest lampposts. On either side, I could see more bridges, and over the balustrade, the picturesque river itself with a few boats on it. Just then, a duck tour passed us with its busload of tourists who would at some point actually float along on the Liffey during their sightseeing. From the Liffey in Dublin to the Thames in London, I never see these living, breathing rivers, with the life of their cities ebbing and flowing through them without wishing, with all my heart, that we could do the same for Mithi and Dahisar, the rivers in Mumbai. All around us were the prominent buildings of the city like the post office, university, and Museum. It all resembled the Fort area of Mumbai with the BMC headquarters and CST railway station.

The wife had a bit of shopping to do for her nephew's two-year-old in London, and we entered the large bookshop, Eason's. I was also hoping to visit the washroom of their café, but at the billing counter, we learnt that the café was closed, being Sunday! Deprived of a visit to a free facility, I turned to Packky and said, "Atta kay" in Marathi (Now what…..literally). This galvanised the girl behind the counter, and she smiled at us and exclaimed, "Oh, you're Marathi." It turned out she was from Kolhapur, was doing her masters in Dublin, and was temping at Eason's while awaiting her results. She was very happy she could chatter in Marathi for a while with us and said that since Dublin had a huge IT sector, that was the reason we had seen lots of Indian faces on the street. She directed us to the Starbucks across the street, right next to the Paddywagon office, which would allow us the free facilities for the price of a coffee, and so we ended our day in Dublin, people watching while P sipped a Pumpkin Spice Latte!

Our slight acquaintance with Dublin reminded us of the group tour, Stars of Europe, that promises to show you twenty cities in ten days. But we did realise that we liked Dublin an awful lot and, that time and other considerations permitting, we would love to make our way here again, via the airport this time and properly "SEE" it! But for now, it was time to go back to our Starship and enjoy our last couple of nights aboard the cruise!

12

Goodbye, Miss Starship

Think of our cruise as a bottle of champagne; we'd popped the Cork, survived the foam and bubbles kicked up by Agnes, and having quaffed it in the Tulip of Dublin, we were now feeling like Irish giants as we strode about the ship on our very last day at sea. We started off the day at Garden Café, where we had seen pyramids of fruits, pastries, different types of bread, and cereals, all these days. Truth to tell, all this vastness and sheer abundance was a little intimidating. Mahindra and Mahindra, at Kandivali, where I had worked for almost a quarter of a century as a medical officer, had these massive canteens, where right from a breakfast of vada pav or Misal Pav to the lunch buffet, then tea, and a smaller workforce coming in for dinner, the massive stoves worked twelve to thirteen hours a day feeding our entire workforce. Similarly, the Garden Café would open even earlier at 5 am for breakfast and at eleven, as soon as the stragglers had finished their breakfast, would set the counters for lunch, then tea, and dinner. Used as we were to the stewards looking after us in the other restaurants, it amused us greatly to see that here, because of the buffet system, they were very eager to clean tables and whisk away plates and dishes rather than serve them. I made sure to guard my plate zealously, as the slightest inattention to a plate would lead to its disappearance in a jiffy, and the table would be sprayed with sanitizer and wiped down! In fact, the Filipino stewards would lurk at the door and spray sanitizer on the hands of all unsuspecting entrants, even if they were patently fresh from the shower. It was by now at least a year and a half since Omicron had sounded the death knell for the COVID pandemic, and yet the scars were all around. Little circles on the floor everywhere admonishing us to maintain distance, sanitizer bottles planted everywhere, and here in Garden Café, where every meal began and ended on this note with frequent punctuations in between of perfumed sanitiser.

This morning, standing at the egg counter, I watched the sous chef separate egg whites and yolks with the efficiency of a surgeon, and the chef beside him cook any type of egg you could possibly ask for - Sunny side up, Poached, Scrambled, Omelette – in the blink of an eye. Watching his artistry while he deftly picked up the egg from the skillet sunny side up without puncturing it and landing it precisely on Packky's plate was almost as mesmerising as eating the final product. Next to him was the cheese counter where the number of cheeses quite boggled my mind. Trying to figure out "kya cheez hai" I sampled a couple of them, and picked up my perfectly toasted brown bread from the conveyor belt of the toaster and seated myself for my 'last breakfast' at a seaside table.

After breakfast, we had planned to complete a very important business of the day, the claiming of the various types of refund that Agnes had made sure the cruise owed us in terms of port fees and excursion fees. Many a time, in malls and department stores, I've stood at the end of a shopping spree, laden with bags, and paid for the privilege of reaching the counter at last. And here was I in a queue where the flow of the lucre was reversed. They were going to pay me when I reached the counter, that too in dollars. I could have stood in such a line all day long. After I'd stood there a while, I felt someone tap my shoulder and turned around to be greeted by 'Savarkar' Guruji and his wife. On the cruise, a few people, by dint of meeting regularly at various lounges and bars and restaurants, had become friendly. We had christened this gentleman Savarkar Guruji as he and especially his beard resembled my Flute Guru, and we had learnt that they resided on the Isle of Wight, a ten-minute ferry ride from Southampton. While we were on our first cruise, they were on their fifteenth and apparently that was because Savarkar Vahini (his wife) couldn't abide flying. Imagine his luck, a wife allergic to flying. Meeting him in the line reminded me that tomorrow when the ship docked at Southampton, Savarkar Guruji would be home within an hour, and it made me homesick for my own home more than 5000 miles away. At last, it was my turn at the counter, and as soon as the girl took down my stateroom number, she handed me a thick wad of dollars in cash saying, "Here's a reward for allowing us to take you on a cruise." Well, it seemed like that anyway.

The wife, on the other hand, was handling a delicate matter. The American cruise line charges you by rote 25 dollars a day as a service charge that is voluntary but never acknowledged as such. Once you figure out that you can and wish to tip whoever you want and the cruise should pay sufficient salaries to the others, you could ask for this back. But apparently, having booked online from the Asia Pacific region, we would have to post the request form to their Sydney office within twenty days. Just FYI, we did so, and we did receive our refund, though they made it an obstacle course to claim it.

Now we were at a loose end having about an hour to go before our spa appointments and done with this most thrilling part of my day, we started off revisiting our favourite places on the ship. At Gatsby's today, a young lady was singing in a beautiful contralto, accompanying herself on the piano. Many a time I'd sat here nursing my Jameson's and watching people. Even after a whole day on land excursions, most of them would dress up to the nines in three-piece suits or jackets as if at a summer wedding, and the ladies in their evening dresses. I wonder, having seen me repeatedly in the same five tee shirts, whether it might have crossed their minds that I had sold the clothes off my back to pay for the cruise. One large group of Gujjus used to be busy chattering among themselves in Gujarati and polishing off the hard corn chakna like sev ganthia as if they were at a picnic spot in Surat. But, while they were too engrossed among themselves, a group of three NRI Indian ladies, I met many times over the last ten days, had talked to me quite a few times. Why she never came across them, was a puzzle to Packky, and why, in spite of not meeting her, the large frog-eyed lady told me 'Your wife is awesome' is a puzzle to me. It must be the rainbow highlights in her silver hair.

Next, we rode the lovely cylindrical glass lift high above the atrium. Today the young Pianist there was accompanied by Paul the vocalist who sang the golden oldies and sported a long goatee tamed by a small rubber band. As we passed the audience, I saw Susan and her husband in a romantic clinch. Susan had her electric chair that allowed her to whizz around the ship despite her mobility issues, and there were many like her, young at heart and determined to enjoy themselves despite their issues. I wished we had more disabled-friendly roads and venues instead of ones with potholes that can immobilise the able-bodied! Another acquaintance of the cruise, Arthur, stepped into the lift at the twelfth floor with his wife and, as was the custom with him, admired Packky's rainbow-coloured hair! How easy Americans are with their friendliness and open admiration of another man's wife. Certainly, more than either us or the Brits. And even if his wife took it like a sport, I would've punched him on the nose if I had to hear him once more.

On our way to the spa, we stopped at the photography station just beside Gatsby's. The three photographers who were always lurking around drumming up business, just like our photographers at

Gateway of India, whether at the grand staircases of the Atrium or the various restaurants, had asked us to choose from our various pictures so that they could print our mandatory copies that came with our 'Romance' package! Just as choosing three sarees necessarily means looking at about sixty, we had to shuffle through fifty seven photos of ourselves at various turns of every staircase, at Le Bistro, and Cagney's in various postures; sometimes a leg curled and an arm awkwardly draped around each other's waist, sometimes she a step above me on the grand staircase, and sometimes some crossing of feet and legs in jigsaw puzzle style! Choosing out of these was an impossible task, but Packky finally narrowed it down to eight and insisted that I should do the final selection. I finally hit upon a simple criterion: I could use these as proof of having carried at least three different t-shirts. With the choice made, the rest of the photos could finally be deleted! After admonishing the photographer to make sure to send the prints to our stateroom by evening, we were on our way to the spa!

Mandara Spa had been attempting to beguile its captive clientele from the ship by various manoeuvres since day one of the cruise. Every day in the cruise newsletter, they published paragraphs on paragraphs in which they promised to perform new miracles... Acupuncture, acupressure, Chinese herbal remedies – all of which would make one look 20 years younger, erase lines under your eyes, and make your skin as plump as it was in your youth – all obvious ploys, geared toward the captive senior citizens! I'd actually fallen for one where Kamal from the gym had done a gait analysis and then tried to hard sell a shoe insert for my flat feet! Their menu had a variety of services from Manicures and Pedicures of various types, wraps and scrubs, aromatherapy, body massage, arm and legs reflexology! While we were waiting for our 'Therapists' to appear, I amused myself with some mental maths converting the dollars, beside these 'therapies', into rupees. Though they sound more and more like doctors, unlike us, they are not afraid to charge astronomical sums, I saw.

Our 'Romance' package offered us a free half-hour Swedish massage, and we had booked it on this, our last day aboard as ideal after traipsing all over Ireland! Soon 3 - 4 of the therapists came forward to greet us and get our forms filled. Now these forms take such a detailed medical history of symptoms, chronic ailments, and whether you have any allergies and such other intimate particulars of your body that if they further took your pulse and blood pressure, they could issue you a medical fitness certificate. Forms out of the way, there came a serious marketing session of any additions to the already purchased service! The seniormost therapist, a Malaysian masseuse named Dolly, took charge of us and began a fifteen-minute tutorial on the benefits of different aromatic oils - variously cinnamon, lavender, rosemary, lemon grass, and ginger. Having no wish to part with the dollars that the cruise ship had just returned to me, I carefully chose lavender as being included in our package and thus managed to irritate her no end! But frankly, lavender was the only aroma I could associate with a massage oil! The rest seemed to be spices used for tea, coffee, or food! Having led us to the couples' therapy room, she left us alone to change and then returned with a junior who took charge of the wife! The room smelt of various perfumed oils, and instead of the usual Bansuri in India, there was a Buddha-Bar tape running faintly in the background! Dolly began to massage the warm lavender oil into my back muscles, all the while explaining how my back was hard, full of knots, how there are lots of irregularities on it that need lots of treatment! As she reached the lower back, she almost made me scream in agony as she discovered and proceeded to annihilate two large knots on either side of my spine! *How*, I thought to myself, *as soon as my back was turned, could my own back stab me in the back and become so knotty... Have you noticed how these people will always depress you... stylists who announce to all and sundry that your hair is thinning, Personal trainers who make sure to let you know how much fatter you are since they saw you last at the gym… You pay these guys to depress you, I guess*! Having survived this marketing session disguised as a massage, I needed the medicinal effects of the Proof Whisky Bar!

As we approached the Proof Whisky Bar, sounds assaulted our eardrums! We had avoided this one like the plague, even though it was named so beguilingly as to offer evidence of the whisky drunk 😊, because it was also the residence of an ongoing Karaoke club. As usual, the most off-key atrocious singers are always lined up, eager to Croak-ke, and even the good whisky could not numb the torture! While the wife checked out the session at Bliss Lounge for further beguiling by the cruise company to hard sell their future cruises, I chose a high stool at the bar and turned my eyes towards the impressive lineup of bottles behind the bar! Alas, my eardrums couldn't join this silent protest! However, when Packky came back with the marketing tales from next door, I felt justified in choosing to sit here as the lesser of the two evils.

We retired to our stateroom to finish our packing and after laying aside the clothes for tonight's gala night at the Stardust Theatre, we settled down to read. She was soon engrossed in her Kindle, but I folded my long frame onto the small ledge of the porthole to stare at the ocean! On open sea, the usual waves and foam we see at the shore are quite absent, and the ocean looked deceptively like a gentle giant pond! It had been our constant companion over the last nine days, at times rosy from the sunrise, at others harsh from the afternoon glare of the sun or ominous and lashing out at Storm Agnes, and at night a vast black brooding presence! This was the real star of this trip. I realised everything else was a mere distraction and silently bowed to this vast force of nature, both in gratefulness and supplication.

The Bliss Lounge changed its character by the hour, somewhat like the Bollywood heroines who change their costumes every 2 seconds during a song sequence! It basically had a bar at one end and a stage at the other. With this basic arrangement, it performed all manner of hard jobs. It was the venue (the bar end) to collect your tickets for tender boats of an early morning before the world awoke, and if that scene wasn't chaotic, it immediately transformed into a fitness class (the stage end). Then at about 10 am, the bar would begin its ritual ablutions of parched throats, and the makeshift chairs would be occupied for some mystery solving or a game of Dumb Charades, or an advertising session for the cruise line's next cruise. However, come evening, the fairy lights and disco strobes came on without fail, the DJ appeared at his turntable, and the bartender was kept busy plying his trade so that all the enthusiastic dancers could give free rein to their 'spirits'. One husband was assiduously plying his wife with wine glasses brimming with love and wine. As all the golden oldies, including a few ABBA and Boney Ms, blasted through the discotheque, I noticed many of the dancers were singing along and wished it was Usha Uthup's Ramba hohoho, or RD Burman and Asha Bhosle's Nisha ahaha ahaha, so I could at least sing along. Our fitness instructor from the cruise director Bianca's team, Maria, from Colombia was dancing along with the guests and encouraging everyone to swing away the night. I was just wondering how she managed to burn the candle at both ends when she spotted Packky and led her, not at all reluctantly, onto the dance floor. Under the strobe lights, P's rainbow-coloured hair seemed to take on a life of its own, and she happily swung to a few numbers before we had to leave for our last show at the Stardust Theatre!

This was how most days on the cruise ended - with either the pre-dinner or post-dinner show! We had watched English magician Michael Charlie Blue's violin recital, Mongolian acrobat juggler Hulan, tightrope walkers and juggling bicyclists, tap dancers, and tonight as a fitting finale, we were going to witness a Parisian Nightclub act, Paradis! Many of the other artistes we had witnessed used to be seen around the ship casually walking around or sitting at the bar! Having watched their impossible physical feats on stage and seeing their lithe physiques up close, obviously at their prime, used to make me suck in my tummy and vow solemnly to myself to make one last push to get rid of 'The Belly' once I was home!

Today, strolling in as if it were our own Borivali's Prabodhankar Natyagruha (theatre), the magic of this giant space on a ship is still undeniable! In fact, one Diwali, we visited Prabodhankar theatre three days in a row, for a Children's Theatre Fest with the kids, and thought we'd overdone it a bit! And here we were visiting 'Stardust' for our 9th day in succession! The French artistes with a veritable smorgasbord of acts created a French Nightclub Act onstage that rivalled the Moulin Rouge in Paris! Simply enthralling!

And as soon as the 'Paradis' troupe wrapped up their act, the entire staff and crew of STAR walked onstage through the various wings! Our cabin attendant Tom, our (by now) old friend Ronny—the restaurant manager, Bianca—the cruise director, and all our fitness instructors from her team, most of whom were Colombian, as well as the captain himself, with a weather-beaten old sailor visage! Spontaneously, the audience rose to their feet and applauded the people who had made our stay so comfortable and entrancing on this floating island!

And so, we were at the end of our cruise, an experience of a lifetime! All that remained was to orchestrate our departure or disembarkation. We had opted for a late slot at 7.30, even though the ship would be docked at 5 am. This was primarily because we had booked a late 11 am train from Southampton to London in case the ship was late and also that our "Romance" package was throwing us its last fruits: breakfast in bed. When we awoke the next morning at 5.15 am, it was to a hubbub of activity outside our porthole. Many of our co-passengers had disembarked, and the ones we saw scurrying down the gangplank were doing so without a backward glance at the ship. Our luggage had been collected the earlier evening by Tom, our backpacks were trussed and ready to go. All that remained was to dress, have breakfast, and depart.

Our trusty 24 one-litre Aqua bottles had trickled out like sand out of an hourglass, and now we had only one left on the shelf above our desk, from which we filled our reusable bottles and then we stood it on the sill of our porthole. So, we looked back from the terminal and said a proper goodbye to the cabin, savouring the last moment from solid ground and waving goodbye to the lone bottle on the sill!

13

Amsterdam

If the cruise was Packky's idea, the wish to visit Amsterdam, without any signs of tulips, might I add, was entirely mine! But before we crossed the Channel to the European continent, there was a load, or several, of laundry to do! Packky chose Jenny's house near Battersea Park specifically because it boasted a washer and a dryer! However, she was clear that guests should not use her dryer! So, we messaged her before booking about our requirements, and she readily agreed to allow us to use both for as many loads as we pleased. Arriving a bit early around noon for check-in, locating the place easily with Jennifer's excellent directions, we made a beeline for the laundry area! Having, with great foresight, packed the clothes needing washing, separately, Packky put the first load in and expertly twirled the knobs to get us a 90-minute cycle! And now, while the clothes cleaned themselves, we'd go out for lunch!

Strolling around the area looking for someplace that would feed us a meal at 2.30 pm, I spotted the local post office and remembered the Service Charge Refund Form I had to post to Australia! But to no avail, Alas! It was shut for the day! Just across from it, we found a small café, and the Barista made us lovely vegan sandwiches with some strange drink to go with it! Gobbling down the sandwiches hungrily (they were delicious), we picked up the drink and hotfooted it back to our pad as it was my turn to get the next load of washing done and to put the washed ones in the dryer!

However, what I found waiting in the laundry was the stuff of my nightmares! Jennifer had pulled our clothes out of the washing machine mid-cycle and loaded her own. She stood there, arms akimbo, demanding to know why we expected to do laundry for a one night's stay!! Here was an accent that I can't understand at the best of times, and an angry Englishwoman looking down her nose and demanding answers. Well, any woman doing it is something I'd much rather never face!

Luckily, of course, I had a secret weapon! Packky came running at my howl for help and with her Airbnb app messages refreshed Jenny's memory about having clarified the need to do several loads of laundry! Magically, it seemed the sight of these messages calmed our hostess, and she agreed graciously that we could continue after her first load was done! It seemed that she managed a couple of BnBs, and today was turnover day for several rooms, so she had loads of work and had clean forgotten what she'd promised us! Packky went along with her to the kitchen and poured oil over the troubled waters as well as offered an olive branch, to mix my metaphors, by petting her Dachshunds!

That evening we went for a long stroll to the large 200-acre Battersea Park! With its gracious green avenues, people walking their dogs, kids rolling by on their scooties at supersonic speed, it was an idyllic scene, and we thoroughly enjoyed walking toward the Pear Tree Café! Settled on a picnic table next to the lake, we watched the evening fall with lots of young women and men with their wine glasses making a merry din! In the midst of it all, an older woman, looking like a dowager countess, walked to a table, put her cane down next to it, and sat down staring at the lake so fixedly she looked like a part of the fixtures! 'I'd like to be like her,' said Packky, 'and stroll down to this lake every evening after I retire!' By now, having heard this sentence ad nauseam, in as varied places as Pondicherry, Rome, Shimla, Athens, I ought to have been used to it! However, I still had to calm my panicked mind by recalling that all it meant was she liked the place an awful lot!

When travelling on your own, without a tour company, all ground transport is a potential for problems, but none more so than an early morning start. However, experienced as she is with booking Ubers from New York to Bali, Packky wasn't too worried that night as we tried to reserve one for 5 am the next morning, to leave for St. Pancras to catch our Eurostar to Amsterdam. But, for some reason, it became mulish and refused to do our bidding! The app wouldn't work on either of our phones and we were in a fix! The glitch seemed to be our credit card payment and while trying to access our net banking, Packky suddenly horrified me, by saying blankly, that she couldn't recall our password! This from my wife who knows all my credit card numbers complete with CVVs and expiry dates, everyone's passport numbers and Pan card numbers and can rattle bank managers by rattling off all numerical information at them! That was a body blow and finally, with no recourse but to approach our host, we timidly called her up at eleven p.m. that night! Thankfully, she went out of her way to calm us and booked her own regular cab driver for us, and besides this, was kindness personified, as she made sure that he had arrived in time, early the next morning, and wished us Godspeed! That was one time I had visions of trudging with our luggage to the station at night and spending the night at St. Pancras!

This was our second experience of the amazing Eurostar that zooms along under the English Channel for 23 miles, cutting the travel time between the two land masses and would take us from London to Amsterdam in a mere four hours! We had in 2010 travelled to Paris by The Eurostar and to further experience the old-fashioned mode of travel, had journeyed back by the P&O ferry to see "The White Cliffs" of Dover!! Despite this, I was mildly surprised to see, that we completed airport-like immigration formalities at the station, and had our bags screened before being allowed into the waiting room! Such is the popularity of this train that even at this early hour, the waiting room was crowded, and I broke into a sweat being warmly dressed against the English autumn outside. I couldn't wait to peel off my jacket as soon as our luggage was stowed on the racks, and we were seated on our comfortable seats!

Though the Channel Tunnel or Chunnel was the great feat associated with it, this is in fact the least interesting part of the journey, as it is all darkness outside! The rest of the journey was filled with delightful, neat scenery as we wandered through France and Belgium en route to Holland. As we entered Holland, some change in the geography or the nature of the houses gave me an inkling of nearing our destination and soon enough, we passed Rotterdam and after a small stop there arrived at Amsterdam Centraal! Spelled with a double A instead of our very own Bombay Central, this station is amazing, flanked by water on both sides - on one side the River Ij and on the other the Centraal Canal! It is more like a posh mall than a railway station and has expensive stores waiting for your custom on all sides! My special travel agent had to collect our three-day pass so we could freely use the tram, metro, bus network throughout the city, from the NS shop or grey-blue and red machine, on the "Ijzide" of the station. So, I herded our bags together and guarding them like a cowherd watched while bicyclists walked into and out of the station with their cycles and as half of Amsterdam seemed to be having their midday coffee at the cafes dotted around! English wasn't the preferred language here and so it was all Dutch to her as Packky attempted to search for the shop that would print our 3-day passes! Having stood futilely in one wrong line at the shop, and another whose printer gave up the ghost as she reached the counter, she finally made them spit out a ticket, that looked remarkably like the old ones in Mumbai, the cardboard ones with tiny printing, and these we would guard jealously, for the next three days of racketing about!

But first we heaved ourselves, bags and all, into a cab at the waterfront, not yet sure whether the vast stretch of water was the Ij or the canal, and took off for our Airbnb at Seinwachterstraat! My mind turns somersaults when setting foot in a new city for the first time! Everything seemed gilded and beautiful - the water in the crisp autumn sunshine, the number of cyclists toing and froing, the vast roads fronting the water everywhere - Ingrid's house seemed to arrive in the blink of an eye! Since we had arrived early, at 12.30 pm when our actual check-in time was 4 pm, which had been kindly advanced by our hostess Ingrid to 2 pm, we were not hopeful about being allowed in. However, with no other recourse, we hoped to be allowed to deposit our bags inside and leave for a leisurely lunch. Our room was a kind of outbuilding to Ingrid's main house, and a narrow passage led to her front door, whose narrowness was further accentuated by a canoe hanging on the wall. Taking care not to knock my bald pate against the canoe, I gingerly approached the front door and rang the bell. No response! Then Packky called Ingrid on her phone, while I strained my ears listening for its ringing inside the house, but to no avail. At last, having messaged her on the app, Packky settled herself to wait on a small bench, hidden from the street by a bunch of greenery in large pots, and I paced the street watching the passersby and in turn being watched by them! Probably I looked like I'd stumbled by accident onto that quiet street of rowhouses overlooking the river!

Just then I heard a loud 'Hello' and a tall Amazon came galloping down the narrow passage from the main house! "I'm Ingrid," she said, wringing my hand so powerfully I immediately realised who rowed the canoe on the wall! She had written on her Airbnb caption that she had grown up swimming in the river Ij! Apologising profusely for having made us wait, she hefted two of our bags into the room and didn't seem to have any inkling that it was we who were early! Over the next few minutes, she pointed out all the devices cunningly placed around the large room! Though it was just one room, it was completely independent with a microwave, refrigerator, ensuite bathroom, and the works! After assuring us that everything in the room was for our consumption, and recommending we try a nearby restaurant—Kanis—for lunch, Ingrid apologised once more and disappeared! On taking stock, we found a month's worth of groceries in the fridge and pantry! Cookies, cold cuts, bottles of juice, cheese, little pats of butter, and to top it off, two big bottles of wine - a red and a white! We had never before, nor have since, been faced with such abundance, and Ingrid will forever be our favourite host - generous and kind, with a heart full of true hospitality!

Deciding to abide by her recommendation, we walked to a restaurant just across the river from Seinwachterstraat on the next island of Java Eiland! Amsterdam on a map looks as if the Irish Giant picked it up in a rage and dashed it down again, shattering it into smithereens, lots of little pieces scattered in the bright waters of the canals which run merrily through it! So, there are about 90 islands and 1500 bridges connecting all these islands! Ingrid had sounded a bit doubtful about whether Kanis would have vegetarian food, having taken for granted that as Indians we would be necessarily vegetarian! However, I was pleasantly surprised to find that the menu was entirely vegan! I felt like I'd expected to be served a chicken Momo and got served a delicious Ukdicha Modak* instead! We settled on a Moroccan broth and a pizza! Then as we waited for our drinks to appear, Packky suddenly darted out, as she spied that they had sidewalk tables!

Sighing, I followed her and happily our beer and wine also made its way out to us almost immediately! "Are those picnic tables across the road also yours?" she asked the waiter and, on his affirming that the riverside tables were indeed theirs, darted across once more and plonked herself with a sigh of satisfaction on one of them, with a long-suffering husband and a mildly amused waiter in her wake! Now, I could enjoy my beer in peace as there was no place to go other than taking a flying leap into the Ij! The Moroccan soup, by the way, was a delicious dal with lots of vegetables and the most delightful spice palette! Using chunks of home-baked bread to dip in and slurping my way to gastronomic heaven seemed like a grand welcome from Amsterdam!

If Mumbai is a city populated by our iconic black and yellow rickshaws and our stray dogs, Amsterdam seemed teeming with cyclists and cats! As we strolled back to our room and crossed over the serpent-like Pythonbrug, a large black and white tomcat casually adopted us and not only accompanied us during our mile-long leisurely stroll but only turned back after seeing us safely to Ingrid's door! And barely were we inside, when a white, heavily scarred cat was rubbing against the glass wall of our room asking to be let in! We had booked a canal boat ride all around the main three canals that afternoon at 4.30 pm to orient ourselves around the city but luckily for me, a siesta had been squeezed into the schedule due to our early start and we snuggled in gratefully on the very comfortable mattress!

Later, refreshed and fortified by a cup of tea, we made our way to the Heineken Center, not for a beer as you might be forgiven for thinking, but because the dock for the canal tour was bang opposite it! Reaching there, involved catching two connecting trams, but was made very easy by the frequency and by screens that accurately foretold the timings of the buses and trams at every stop!

The tour itself was not more than half full that afternoon, and we settled ourselves in, with our audio guides, telling us in various languages, all the rich and varied history of the city and the individual buildings or streets, as we passed them. The coordination—between the captain's navigation and the commentary—was remarkably in sync. The seventeenth century was the Dutch Golden Age where its trade with the Balkans, along with its spice trade with the Far East, bore fruit, and Amsterdam began long years of huge immigration waves. In order to make commerce easy and to allow for the expansion of the city, the canal system was built in a fan shape from west to east, rather like the swathe of a windshield wiper. The large ones, Herengracht, Keizergracht, and Prinsengracht, were the semicircular canals that began and ended in the Ij and had multitudinous smaller canals and bridges joining them. Today they are mainly used for tourism, houseboats, and recreation.

The canal walls had large iron chains, to pull boats in and tie them up, that looked so old, they transported me three hundred years back. The noblemen and rich tradesmen built huge narrow-fronted mansions along the main canals, and today these residences have turned into corporate offices, which, however, have only discreet nameplates, such that the houses still retain the look and flavour of private residences. The narrow fronts, by the way, are a tax-saving ploy from the days long gone as the Dutch were taxed according to the area of the wall fronting the canal so the houses are sometimes huge inside but boast a narrow front profile for the oldest of reasons—to save on municipal taxes! One of the great sights was an old ship, belonging to the erstwhile Dutch East India Company-VOC! This looked straight out of The Pirates Of The Caribbean movie, complete with a replica Pirate as the figurehead! This ship, which was called "The Amsterdam", has been lovingly restored and is moored along the National Maritime Museum. Even if most of its parts have been replaced making it more Ship of Theseus than The Amsterdam, their great desire to preserve their history drew my admiration!

When the canals narrow down as they often do, making it difficult for two boats to pass each other, our captain politely reversed, to speed the other on its way! It reminded me of Himachal, where the narrow mountainous terrain makes such manoeuvres both necessary and hair-raising! During one such halt, I looked around the boat at our fellow passengers for the first time. There was an Arab family of four on the table ahead and a Korean couple behind us. Besides these, there were just a group of five friends chatting at the very rear of the boat. Surprisingly, Packky decided to use the washroom at the back of the boat, but as she made her way there, the Korean guy emerged from it and shamefacedly asked her to refrain as he had a bad tummy and had just used it! Now, Packky's ideas of what a loo should be are legendary they should be pristine, chalk dry, and smelling of lavender fields for a start! Recounting to me, with horror, her near miss, she was almost sick, just at the thought of it! And so, having abruptly time-travelled from history to the rude present, we disembarked and made our way into the Heineken Experience to discuss the possibility of a tour the next day and, more importantly, to use their washrooms!

The Heineken Office had closed for the day, but the staff assured us that we could walk in for a tour the next day and kindly ushered us to the washrooms. On our way out, we passed through an atrium with their entire history illustrated on large panels! Gerard Heineken bought a small brewery in 1873 called The Haystack, gave his family name to it, and began producing premium lager! The rest, as they say, is history! Having spent an absorbing ten minutes reading their history, we decided we knew all we wanted to, about it, and the rest could be deciphered by multiple tasting sessions over the next few meals! Saved us 40 euros, that washroom break!

We emerged to a lovely evening in Amsterdam; there were gardens all around and, even this late in the season, masses of colourful flowers in tubs everywhere! This is the perfect time your tongue and teeth demand to be fed, along with your other senses! And right after the bridge, what should we come across, but a hot-dog cart! These are as frequent in the west as vada pavs and bhelwala gadis (carts) are at home. Filled with hot mustard sauce that travels straight up your nose to heat and possibly burst through the top of your head with lots of onions, pickles, and tomatoes, it's the ideal snack for such an evening! The cart owner, meanwhile, was doing all he could to lure us there, as yet having no customers! As soon as he heard we were Indians, he bellowed, "Aahh India!" and then asked Packky to guess his country of origin. After a few futile guesses of Spain, Portugal, etc., he announced, "I'm from Podgorica, Montenegro", a country I had barely heard of, leave alone its capital, which was totally unknown to me. Packky was enthusiastically discussing the breakdown of erstwhile Yugoslavia with him, while I mulled over this piece of information! Way back in 2018, when we travelled to Iceland, we had an irritating fellow passenger, a girl who would forget her personal items on the bus and had to go back for them every so often, delaying our guided tour. Interestingly though, we learnt she hailed from Suriname, which has a sizeable Indian-origin population and where Hindi is one of the languages they are expected to learn at school! This was due to migration of indentured labour brought by the Dutch to Suriname. Coincidentally, beginning in the year 1873, the year Gerard began Heineken production in Amsterdam! Now, I mused if I came here with Raj Travels or Kesari Tours, I'd get Indian food, it's true! But the living geography that I experienced in the form of Montenegro and Suriname would be something lost, as P is always at great pains to explain to me!

The next morning, we visited the panoramic lookout at A'DAM Tower, though true to form, we didn't try the daredevilry of their aerial swing! I can never fathom why having your heart in your mouth, and reducing your lifespan, sounds so exciting to a lot of people! Count me out! Then we had an unplanned morning, wandering around Amsterdam, seeing the VOC ship up close, sipping wine while watching cruise ships docked at their harbour! This last was particularly interesting, as we had just hopped off a cruise, and we both agreed on our earlier opinion that you never connect with the land destinations when visiting as a day tripper from the ship! Take Amsterdam, for example! Unless, you walk the streets for a couple of days, and are run down by their cyclists at least a couple of hundred times, perfecting several manoeuvres, jumps, and agonised yelps, as you find them bearing down on you, you would never know it! It is simply a city of cyclists, all manners of them! Large and small, with baskets and boxes and sidecars attached to them for various goods like groceries, pots of plants, large gunny bags of cement, and planks of wood, several dogs and cats in permanent residence in them! Similarly, their riders are of all ages, shapes, and sizes! They never seem to walk anywhere but just throw one leg over the bar and take off on this ubiquitous two-wheeler! They cycle alone, with a friend, chatting as they ride side by side, or in boisterous droves! As we cross roads, we're actually crossing over one road for motorists, one track for trams, and another for cyclists, right next to the pedestrian track! A most dangerous placement as the motorists might politely wait while you cross over, in fact do, but the cyclists will as soon knock you down as look at you! As the entire responsibility, to avoid them, is on the pedestrian, they never bother to ring their cycle bells, which is a courtesy even tram drivers afford you before squashing you flat!

After another leisurely lunch at Kanis and another siesta, we set out in the early afternoon to visit the Rijksmuseum! In the last thirty-five years of travelling, if there's one trigger for me, it's the word Museum! Churches and cathedrals are somewhat in this category but at least afford a restful bench to sit at and the possibility of heavenly music, as well as the surety, that apart from a couple of candles, there will be no needless purchase! Museums are up there in a category of their own! Over the years, I have walked many miles down the long endless corridors of a long endless list of museums - The Louvre, Musee d'Orsay and Orangery in Paris, New York's MOMA and the

Natural History Museum, The Uffizi and Academia in Florence, the Red Cross Museum in Geneva, the Acropolis Museum and the Benaki in Athens, and on and on… watched the thousands of people walking by the mind-numbing array of paintings, sculptures, arms and armaments, clothes, jewellery, furniture, light fixtures... in short, anything that someone would certify as authentically old! I've barely saved myself from falling into a permanent coma at the sight of so many objects clumped together! In contrast, visiting Academia to see Michelangelo's David and visiting Milan for the Last Supper as a lone painting seems infinitely preferable! So I had a deal with Packky, that I would not risk stepping into The Rijks! Instead, I sat outside in a garden, resembling the Tuileries, with a small pond and plenty of sand scattered all over to give the illusion of a beach, to those who spent the summer in the city! Occupied by my favourite sport, people watching, I observed a young woman come cycling in to meet up with a young man, seated two benches away from me! They talked for a couple of minutes and then she slipped a ring off her finger and cycled away! No drama! Now what happened here? Did she hand over the ring for fitting or did she break a long-standing engagement? There was no way I could read their emotions, as I was quite far-off and so, your guess is as good as mine! And now, having made sure to click a few good photos with the Rijksmuseum as a backdrop, I could wholeheartedly assure everyone that it has a great collection of Vermeers, Rembrandts and Van Goghs! I might even, at a pinch, discuss the composition of 'The Night Watchman' for a couple of minutes! 😊

Bollywood released a movie called "QUEEN" in 2013, which had nothing to do with any kind of royalty or Freddie Mercury! It was the story of Rani, a simple Delhi girl, in itself a conundrum, who, having been jilted at the altar, continues on her long-cherished honeymoon trip to Paris and Amsterdam, all on her own. The solo trip helps change her perspective, that marriage should be the be-all and end-all of her existence! Now, I'm well aware that this movie did wonders for the actress Kangana Ranaut and performed excellently at the box office because we were personally responsible for a majority of its collections! Packky loved it so much that after we'd watched it, she'd shanghai anyone who she could and take them to the movie - her staff, her anaesthetist, her mother, aunt, uncle, maybe the neighbours...and even today if she's having a hard day, she'll put it on Netflix, fall asleep at the first song "London Thumakda", and wake up cheerful again!

On this solo trip, Rani/Queen visits Amsterdam and stays in dormitory-like accommodation booked by her friend Vijay! Here she makes friends with three guys, and they accompany her to the red-light district to hand over a parcel to Rukhsar, a commission she was executing for Vijay. Uncomfortable in the area, she locates Rukhsar, but has difficulty introducing herself, as Rukhsar mistakes her for a client at first! On her expressing shock at this mode of earning money, Rukhsar pragmatically says, "Well, when I send money home, it's finally just money." When we hesitantly decided to visit the district, we had no idea what we'd find there! Having seen Mumbai's ill-famed Shuklaji street, in passing, several times, I wasn't expecting this to be any different. As we approached the area, the pleasant, wide, tree-lined avenues of Amsterdam got progressively narrower and took on a seedy character, that seemed befitting! The iron railings on the canal walls were rusting, and many rusted discarded cycles were piled in heaps on the canal banks! The narrow lanes leading in were lined with shops, boasting luridly lit-up signposts, many of them selling weed, sex toys, and the like! One hot pink neon light boldly announced Sex Shop, which incongruously made us giggle nervously!

Now, the lanes became narrower and very crowded! The men around seemed to get boisterous, and my, usually intrepid, wife decided to hold my hand! Prostitution is legalised and licensed in this district of Amsterdam, and so is any shop selling pornography, marijuana, and other generally illegal stuff. The shops displayed their licences boldly outside, and keeping one hand protectively on my money belt, we proceeded down tiny streets reminding me of Kalbadevi! Guru Dutt's powerful movie Pyaasa with its iconic song "Jinhe naaz hai Hind pe woh kahaan hai" kept playing in my mind as a kind of background music to this scene! The air was perfumed by the sweetish smell of weed as we stood near a shop proclaiming "Smoke Shop Seed Bank Official Dealer," when, all of a sudden, I saw a beautiful young girl, who could barely have been about 17 or 18 if at all. Scantily clad, she stood beckoning the passerby in a garishly lighted window, like a strangely live mannequin. Her profession had still not snatched away the lovely innocence on her face, and I thought how differently she would appear to us if we met her on the street, clad in jeans and a t-shirt, some morning, with a group of her friends. While I stood lost in this reverie, almost but not quite leaning on the wall behind me, a sudden movement at the corner of my field of vision made me whirl around in alarm! This too was a display window, and the lady, of indeterminate age who stood here, had obviously been jaded and ravaged by time. It wrung my heart, to feel that at one time, she might have been just like the youngster at the opposite window, and as if with one mind, we scurried out of the area, as if all hell's hounds were after us. Fittingly, we lost our way out and had to traverse a dark lonely alleyway before finding our way to the tram stop, and Packky would not stop, even, to check her trusted Google Maps on the way.

Before we had entered the precincts of Rijksmuseum earlier, at the main crossing, we had been delighted to observe a large placard advertising an Indian restaurant called the Madras Diaries!! Very proud of this compatriot who had the muscle power to advertise in this prominent location, we had made up our minds to return here for dinner. So, we took the bus back and with some difficulty located it in a street full of international cuisine! The difficulty was that it was located on the first floor of Lange Leidsedwarsstraat, 37-41, and that seemed to befuddle Mr. G Maps completely! We found we were lucky to snatch a recently vacated table as it was chock-full of people, completely booked up, and not just by Indian tourists! There were many locals who seemed to know our host and his stewards well and have favourites on the menu! That night I went a little crazy and ordered chicken barotta, koru ghee roast, palak paneer chemeen biryani with A madras mule and a Pondicherry Punch! To top it off, we had a Gulab Jam and a gulab milk! Of course, we couldn't finish it all but the rest was lovingly packed into tiffins for the next night's dinner! I can honestly say that it was one of the best Indian meals I have ever had.

Zaanse Schans is a special area 15 km north of Amsterdam that is earmarked for the preservation of history! At one point in the seventeenth century, there used to be more than 600 windmills in the entire northern area! When windmills became nonfunctional, they were transported by lowboy trailers to this little village and can be visited here! They have picturesque names such as The Cat, The Houseman, The Seeker, and a couple are still to be found in the same place that they were built in the sixteenth century. Other than these few windmills, there are, concentrated in a very small, circumscribed area, a workshop cum shop for Scholls--the iconic wooden shoe from Holland, and a cheesemaking workshop demonstrating the process and selling Gouda cheese, along with what seemed to be a million souvenir shops! To put it succinctly, a tourist TRAP! We were only lured into it because there's almost no other way to see the old windmills! So, we watched while a taciturn old man made a wooden shoe in one minute! If he was making a shoe a minute, for the millions of tourists day in and day out and being asked the same ridiculous questions, he had every right to be permanently enraged and he was!! I was mortally afraid of our already swollen bags exploding with the addition of wooden shoes but mercifully only a small wooden fridge magnet made it home with us! Next, we watched while every herb and condiment made its way into Gouda cheese and of course it was too much to hope for, not buying one roundel of each kind! On our way back, our lady bus driver gave us some interesting information about the canals! Apparently, all of Holland is below sea level and, to drain the excess water from the ground, multiple canals are the best of all options. Another pithy comment of hers was, easily, the most amusing thing I heard during the trip! She said, "Don't let the people of Amsterdam fool you into thinking, they ride cycles for the environment, or to avoid sound pollution! They are misers and ride cycles to avoid large fuel bills." The entire group burst into laughter and we reached her city a few moments later.

If there was one focus for Packky in Amsterdam, it was the Anne Frank Museum. There are some non-negotiable visits, such as The Last Supper in Milan, that she swears she's spent a lifetime wanting. And the availability of tickets for these is always poor. I remember how one Tuesday, in 2017, two months before visiting Italy, we were hunched over our laptops, making sure to book Da Vinci's world-famous scrawl on a dining room wall, and we managed it too! This time around, however, we had to pay a hefty premium to an online intermediary, to lay our hands on the tickets to the Anne Frank memorial on Prinsengracht! The Frank family were well-to-do Jews in Amsterdam, who were forced into hiding due to the Nazi takeover of Holland, and there they stayed in quarters approached through a narrow bookcase on the second floor of Anne's father's office building! The next day, as we joined crowds of tourists in the line for our entrance hour, and watched them sipping their Starbucks coffees and chatting, it hardly seemed possible, that this place had seen two families undergo such privation for two years, before being unfortunately betrayed and caught on 4th August 1944, just days before the Armistice! Anne was taken to the Bergen-Belsen concentration camp, where she tragically met her untimely end!

As we entered the Westermarkt, the house fronting on Prisengracht, we were asked to deposit our backpacks at the counter and, were given an audio guide with headphones before being ushered into the museum. Every room had photographic and written records of Anne, her family, the Van Pels family who were incarcerated with them, Miep Gies, her husband Jan, Johannes, Victor Kugler, and Bep Voskuijl who helped them by bringing in essential items such as groceries, so they could survive! Each display had a number, which played the relevant commentary, when the audio guide was held close to it! Increasingly uncomfortable and rendered mute by both the human suffering and the human violence casually displayed on these walls, it was a silent line that inched forward! There is an inherent dissonance, about tourists on a vacation, having an absolutely lovely time in a free world, being abruptly faced with the price that others have paid and still continue to pay in some parts of the world, for this freedom! And this was further accentuated, as one by one we squeezed through the door behind the narrow bookcase and entered their living quarters! Anne, her sister, parents, and another six people lived in the two rooms we now entered! Many of their things have been left as they are, including their kitchen platform, sink with its brass tap, and a few vessels! The red diary, in which the young teenager scribbled her innermost thoughts, including a crush for the Van Pels boy, is also on display! Otto Frank, Anne's father, the only one of all of them to finally survive and return, got the diary from Miep Gies and published it posthumously as 'Diary of a Young Girl'! It has, since, made its way into the hearts of millions and has been translated into many languages! Its popularity has turned the house into one of the shrines evoking the Holocaust victims!

All the racketing around the world had left us physically tired, but now we felt a soul-deep exhaustion, which had nothing to do with the travails of our journey. Every penny forked out for this seemed worthwhile! We bought another copy of Anne Frank's Diary to remember this visit and collapsed on the deep chairs of the café. Staring out of the window at the sun setting on the canals, the pretty picture seemed incongruous to our eyes, but a reviving cup of coffee and a shared apple pie, helped reconcile us to our privilege!

And, now, it was time to bid goodbye to Amsterdam, a city that I had developed a sneaking fondness for, in the three days that I had been there! We had traversed Seinwachterstraat so many times, that it seemed like home! Two doors away from Ingrid's, sat a large clay image of Ganpati just outside someone's door! Delighted, to find our favourite deity had followed us to a foreign land, we paid obeisance to Him every time we passed! Today we plucked a blood-red flower looking very much like His favourite, the hibiscus, and laid it at his feet as a goodbye!

And we were off to London as a last stop en route to finally going where I longed to be—Home!!

14

London

Packky, to her infinite regret, didn't have control over our very first trip together, our honeymoon! In the time-honoured fashion and the tradition of my family, my father Appa wrote a postcard to Mr. Sahastrabuddhe of Girivihar in Mahabaleshwar and sent him a money order booking us in for 8 days! It was an all-inclusive package with a set menu for every day of the week, and when we ate the first day's set menu again, we knew it was time to go home!! To add insult to injury, the food was exclusively pure vegetarian, Maharashtrian (read Kokanastha) food, which offended the rabidly non-vegetarian Goan who can't imagine dining out on a vegetarian menu. And so it began, our cruise through life, travelling from opposing points of view, towards a possible compromise.

Needless to say, every subsequent journey has seen Packky firmly holding the reins! Left to my own devices, I would've done the standard circuits of Lonavala, Matheran, Mahabaleshwar, and a little further afield like Shimla-Kullu-Manali, or Bangalore-Mysore-Ooty! In truth, when Packky asks the dreaded question, "So, where shall we go?" my heart cries, "Nowhere! I want to stay HOME!" and every time she hears that, she says, "Well, we do stay home almost 280 days in a year." She was born with wheels on her feet; she enjoys every aspect of travelling! Whether it's getting lost, getting rained in, or having to abandon three ports to escape the Storm Agnes! Her reaction to watching the frightening wave lash our porthole was,

"Well, how many people get to experience a storm while on a cruise?" So, perforce I cudgel my brains for long-forgotten geography lessons and come up with places like the "Leaning Tower of Pisa" when we went to Italy and windmills this time when I realised, to my surprise, that we were going to wander the continent after our cruise! Any sane person (read: I) would have flown home from Southampton or maybe tacked on a day or two in London after an eleven-day cruise racketing around Ireland! But who can stop Packky, the whirlwind? She considers the carbon footprint of a transcontinental flight wasted unless she spends three weeks there. Given a choice, actually three months, but having to leave Maia behind, rather puts paid to that.

So, on any given trip I'm pretty clueless about the itinerary and if on being told at the airport that instead of Iceland we're catching a flight to Finland it wouldn't matter a whit! This trip too, I had exasperated her several times, when in Amsterdam, by asking "Are we in Holland and will be going to the Netherlands!" But of all the countries in the world, if she were forced, under great duress, to choose just one to travel to, the United Kingdom would win hands down! I grew up reading Faster Fene, P.L. Deshpande and G.A. Kulkarni and they populate my imagination with people and places in and around Pune and Mumbai! But, having read only Enid Blyton, Agatha Christie, Georgette Heyer, Bill Bryson and Jane Austen, her dear old England populates her dreams! The first time she travelled by the tube in London, she felt like the stations of Covent Garden, Trafalgar Square, Piccadilly Circus, Baker Street were more familiar than Mahalaxmi and Mumbai Central. So, she bats for spending a few days in London, every time we are flying out of Heathrow.

The British, having colonised us for over 150 years, continue to torture us further by having us fill their visa form. Since a British visa would enable us to visit Ireland as well, it was inevitable! Besides three years of income tax returns, we had to submit every conceivable financial document you own, your great grandmother's jewellery, your family tree stretching seven generations, and the address of every relative in the UK alive or dead! That's all that you have to provide in the form! To avoid having to do this every other year, we researched and filled this form online and manually, and forked over half of my Provident fund, to apply for a ten-year visa! Now, the crux here, is that they get to keep the money even if they refuse the visa, so after a tense wait of ten days, when it finally arrived, we heaved a collective sigh of relief!

And that is how on a sunny autumn morning, we arrived at Vauxhall in a cab from St. Pancras intending to spend our last four days here! Our cab, guided by Google Maps, stopped at a small four-storeyed apartment building with large old-fashioned balconies! As we rang our host to ascertain the floor of our apartment, a tall man peeped over the balcony on the top floor and bellowed, "Hi, I'm Ti! Come on up!" Mentally groaning at the thought of climbing the stairs, laden with our now puffed-up luggage, I entered the building only to find Ti had galloped down and effortlessly lifted our two largest bags, then galloped up again! Following sheepishly in the wake of so much energy, we brought up the remaining luggage and deposited it in the room Ti indicated! And now when she began to explain all the rules of her apartment to us, it dawned on me that Ti was our hostess. Wearing baggy track pants, a checkered bright green shirt with a collar, and sporting a crew cut with a cowlick at the top, I could be forgiven for mistaking her gender initially. She was very stern about her check-in and check-out timings, so until 4 pm we were only allowed to drop our luggage in the apartment, for which concession we were devoutly thankful. Otherwise, an extremely friendly person, we knew in those first ten minutes of introduction that she was a divorced mother of three, a grandmother twice over, and an Operating Room staff nurse at the nearby St. Thomas Hospital. Showing us around the place, she explained that she would leave the keys in a lockbox downstairs after her cleaning service finished and messaged us the code to it! And now we were free to proceed to London's great attraction – Packky's nephew Rituraj and his 3-year-old daughter Sakshi!

That evening, being a Sunday, Rituraj and his wife Vanaja had planned on taking us to Hampstead Heath! Just a few kilometres from central London, the heath is a 790-acre wild park full of woods and meadows perched on a hill affording a view of all of London! It's a favourite haunt of Londoners on a weekend, to picnic, to walk their dogs and kids and meet their friends, and this Sunday, it made me feel for one moment as if I was a resident myself! There are houses at the edge of the park that are so wildly expensive they are the privilege of today's noblemen, the financial moguls. Having strolled around for a while, we repaired to Ritur's favourite pub there, "The Spaniard's Inn." Entertaining Sakshi and chatting with Ritur and Vanaja gave me a warm feeling of home, after having wandered among strangers over the last few weeks! It was a balmy autumn evening, and yes, I know I keep saying this, but the English weather was behaving beautifully and so deserves a better reputation.

The Spaniard's Inn itself, built in 1585 by two Spanish brothers, is steeped in history! Perched at the edge of the heath near Hampstead village, it is said to have been the regular haunt of literary giants like Charles Dickens and John Keats. They even have plaques saying ** was here, at some upstairs tables, that Ritur insisted on taking me to see! More interestingly, The Spaniard's Inn is said to be haunted by the highwayman Dick Turpin and his horse Black Bess. Looking at its old polished wooden beams, uneven floor, and its dark wood panelling, I could see they made a compelling, cosy but spooky ambience.

The next day we woke up late because today we had the luxurious morning of "The Unplanned Day". Having returned late last night, we at first decided to take stock of our little suite. Little, was the operative word here, as there was a tiny bathroom which, since it was fitted with a bathtub, had barely room for my limbs, a tiny toilet half the size of the bath, and our mid-size bed-sitting room, which perforce was the largest room of the three! As if to make up for their lack of size, they were eclectically decorated! The toilet had a large book with 365 shlokas in Sanskrit, one presumably for every day you sat on the pot. Besides this, the walls had posters of a rock band, of a Mamma Mia stage show on Broadway, and other small wooden knick-knacks hung on the walls on tiny nails! I used to be terrified of knocking something over in that small space! The bathroom had a colourful décor of 6" by 6" tiles, sourced from all over the world - Portuguese Azulejos, mixed in with Sevilla tiles and many others which, try as I might, I can't remember, as I know nothing about ceramics! One morning while listening to the ruckus from the neighbouring Vauxhall school I accidentally dislodged the shower head which had been tied with plastic twine to the pipe! After I tied it back I made sure to never touch it again even if it meant not washing my back for a couple of days!

But this morning our dilemma was to do with a tea kettle or rather its absence! On ringing the bell next door, which was Ti's home, she told us some erstwhile guest had short-circuited her wiring by allowing the kettle to burn to a cinder, and so she had stopped providing one! It took all our combined sweet persuasion for her to grudgingly hand over the electric kettle and cups. Relieved, we drank several extra cups of tea and lazed around before finally making our way to Hyde Park.

Newly married in 1989, my young wife was posted at St. George's Hospital V.T., where she was on duty almost 24/7 as a junior resident. I had often visited her quarters, and Sterling Cinema had been our favourite haunt for movies, like Bruce Willis' *Die Hard* series. Once, while dining at the restaurant Hyde Park, opposite Sterling, she had mused aloud, "Do you know, that this is named after the famous park in London? I'm definitely going there someday!" As it happened, I didn't know, and neither did I hear the faint warning bells of my future travel. Even though, I had not yet awarded her the sobriquet 'Packky', she was showing me the entire future, in a crystal ball, with just that one dreamy sentence.

Placed in the borough of Westminster, the 350-acre Hyde Park, one of London's 3000+ parks, is a jewel! Open year-round with a great political history of free speech and debate at Speaker's Corner, it is an oasis of peace and calm surrounded as it is by the hubbub all around it! Maintained beautifully over the last 400 years, divided by the Serpentine from Kensington Park, Princess Di's fiefdom, it would need a week to explore fully. When we wandered barefoot on the grass, there were plenty of people here. But somehow the vastness of it gave everyone seclusion and a feeling of privacy. We found a great big oak tree and flung ourselves down on the grass carpeted with fallen leaves. Warmed by the weak autumn sun, we lazed around marvelling at our luck with the weather. That silent half-hour, with the London traffic just a faint buzzing of a bumblebee in the background,was more refreshing than any spa day for sure! Anywhere on earth, the ground beneath and the skies above are absolutely the same, and that musing was like temple bells ringing in my head! As if to confirm my philosophy, I saw a man on my right having spread his prayer shawl on the ground, praying in the direction of Mecca! On my left, an artist had set up his easel and was engrossed in his Plein Air sketching! In the middle of this great theological stream of thought, came a demand to photograph the scene from all angles, and it dawned on me why Rishi Munis needed to retire to the Himalayas for meditation. Shaking off my reverie and interrupting this communion with myself, I was marched off to visit the Frameless Exhibition near Marble Arch.

The guy at the counter was telling a couple of girls ahead of us, that they would get the tickets for 20 pounds online, while at the window they were charging 32 pounds! The girls immediately huddled to one side and we were at the counter! When he took one look at us and asked us how many tickets we wanted, Packky demanded the same info he had just given the girls! He smirked, obviously not believing she could get anything online and repeated the information! She immediately registered herself on the site, requiring an OTP from Ritur as they needed a local number! Having got our tickets, she then kindly guided the youngsters to complete their purchases, and revengefully smirked back at the ticketing clerk! I suspect half the fun of travelling, is getting to use her phenomenal tech skills.

On entering the exhibition, I must, shamefacedly, confess that I made a beeline for the cafeteria! I'm not a person with much appreciation for art and how, I managed to have children who are both good artistes, is a mystery to me. Besides, I do believe that a full stomach is more conducive to the appreciation of the finer things in life! Having whiled away an hour and a quarter, we entered the first room at 5.15 pm, and the closing time was 6 pm! I considered 45 minutes plenty for any exhibition and had my philistine notions blown away by an immersive experience of Surrealism! The art, that on flat canvases never seemed to touch me, was now projected on any and all surfaces of the room, including the spectators. Dali's clocks melted all over my person in A Persistence of Memory, and fantastic figure of The Fireside Angel by Ernst cavorted on the walls, enjoying a picnic, in The Garden of Earthly Delights by Bosch. Fantastical beasts, human-animal hybrids, huge Amazonian vegetation, all seemed to move and surround me, until I was eventually steeped in it. Many people sat cross-legged on the floor watching the show unfold, and I joined them, wanting to enjoy the experience fully. We got so lost in the experience we spent almost half an hour in this one room, and only when we walked out, did we realise that it had six other rooms, which, we then perforce, hurried through!

The room with the Monet and Van Gogh interpretations took up some time, and we hurried into the last Impressionists' room at 5.59 pm, prepared to leave after a cursory glance! However, strolling through Canaletto's Piazza San Marco, and gasping at Rachel Ruysch's Tree trunk surrounded by flowers, butterflies, and animals, held us in the room beyond closing time! Two officials now entered and began ushering us out, and as we resolutely turned our back on the room, we were suddenly back on the cruise watching Storm Agnes! This last one, was Rembrandt's 'Christ in the Storm on the Sea of Galilee'. Accompanied by lightning and thunder, the full fury of the storm burst upon us, and we watched, in horror and with all our sympathy, the sailors of yore. Now, it's possible that purists will not agree, but I do encourage everyone, to experience immersive art at least once, to see if they can appreciate these great artists, to some small degree!

As a teenager, travelling from Girgaon to Elphinstone College, I had always caught the Double Decker Bus No. 135 and sat at the very front of the Top Deck! Full of future plans and dreams, those journeys over two of the most crucial years in our education system, still hold a soft spot in my heart. Now, BEST has phased out most of their double deckers, but London's historical bus system, running continuously since the nineteenth century, still has them. Running more than 600 routes, the buses cover almost every bit of the city thoroughly, and we had decided to enjoy as many of them as possible. The very first time we visited, we stayed with our niece in Virginia Waters, and though it was an idyllic spot to stay in, exploring London meant taking the train every day to Waterloo. Rather like exploring Mumbai from Palghar. This time around, Vauxhall being a great hub for transport, we took buses everywhere, to Hyde Park, to Ritur's place near Paddington, to Trafalgar Square, to Liberty and Selfridges, and Covent Garden. Vanaja had told us to use our credit cards on the readers without buying any separate transport cards. Using contactless, the daily cap of £5.25 meant that after three rides, we weren't charged, and this delighted me no end. The one sticking point here is some machines would randomly refuse some cards, and on hearing the peculiar high pitch of refusal, we'd scramble for another one. Watching the drivers in these circumstances was a study in human nature! Being notoriously in a hurry to complete their route on time, some of them grimaced and made disgruntled noises, some barked at us, while still others wearily waved us into the bus, not wanting the irksome wait, until one of our cards hit the sweet spot!

The route to Ritur's home was our most frequented, and we felt we recognised a driver after a couple of days. This route passed through Edgware Road, which is populated by Egyptians, Iraqis, and Arabs and has long been full of shisha bars, halal shops, and restaurants! Passing every day through this area, crowded and full of colour and movement, the air perfumed by ittar and spicy kebabs, it took me back to Mohammed Ali Road outside JJ Hospital where I had my medical training. Known as Little Cairo or Little Beirut by Londoners, on 7th October it seemed remarkably quiet, and the shop fronts were all shuttered! "Maybe it's closed on Saturday," we said to ourselves, but when we reached Ritur's home that day, he was big with the news of the Hamas' terrorist attack on Israel, and he refused to allow us to go back by bus, making sure of it, by calling us an Uber himself. Somehow this disturbing event, a portent of a roiling, violent Middle East, brought us out of the vacation world into the real world, as nothing else could have! By silent consensus, we hadn't been following the news closely, accentuated by having very little data on the ship. It had felt good to be isolated for a while, but now we were back, literally with a bang, and were obsessively following the newspapers again!

We might avoid the usual tourist haunts of London such as the London Eye, Buckingham Palace, Tower Bridge, or St. Paul's (the only church I'm genuinely fond of because of its dome), but no matter how many times we come back, we're never going to avoid Harrods or Selfridges, Liberty or Primark! I have only one word for the prices of stuff in Harrods – HORRIBLE! It's like capitalism on steroids, with everything having an inflated price absolutely disconnected from its value. Noticing, that the price of a stringy pair of sandals on one of the mannequins was above one lakh, made me wonder whether I'm going to be charged for the horror of having laid eyes on them. The absolute quiet with no signs of any customer reinforced my belief, however baseless, that they had overreached themselves and were due for a fall.

Stepping from here to Primark, is like stepping into Sahakar Bhandar after leaving a mall. There were long lines at the cash counters, befitting the ration store lines in Mumbai once upon a time, and all the Pakistani and Bangladeshi clerks at the counter were kept very busy! However, it was necessary to join the queue, as one of her hospital staff had requested Packky to buy some cosmetics for her sister's parlour in Pune! So, I went trailing behind, in her wake, as she strolled down aisles of eyeshadow and blush palettes, not for the first time bewildered that such things are needed by anyone, leave alone the pragmatic women of Pune.

And now, the very last of Packky's idiosyncrasies – we've never gone to London and not spent our last day or two in Windsor. The love affair began at the very first visit, when we were at Virginia Waters and had visited Windsor Castle and its deer park, almost as soon as we set foot in England. This time, however, due to my veto, we had no plans to visit and definitely no plans to stay. But, when she woke the last morning with a wistful look in her eyes, I capitulated and we set off for the erstwhile Queen's home! Catching the direct SW Railway train from Vauxhall, we wound our way past Clapham Junction, Putney, Richmond, Twickenham, and Staines to Windsor and Eton (Riverside). There were hardly any passengers on the train this morning, and we luxuriated in choosing to sit at two separate windows with the entire carriage at our disposal. On alighting, we found that we were among a total of eight foot passengers and two cyclists on the train down from London.

Windsor is one of the two small pretty twin towns of Windsor and Eton (of the famed boys' school), connected by the Windsor Bridge, over the River Thames. A quiet little royal borough, this comely town has neat shops, clean streets, and had not a whiff of traffic on this quiet Wednesday. Walking up to the castle from the station, we went down a small lane with the residences of the palace staff on either side and the centuries-old St. George's Chapel. Before we knew it, we arrived at the gates of the large park facing the castle, at the top of The Long Walk. This three-mile-long walk is a straight ceremonial avenue, created within the deer park, to serve as a grand entrance and has seen many royal processions and ceremonial parades! It ends on Snow Hill at The Copper Horse, a statue of King George III astride on a horse, which not only provides a focal point while walking down the avenue but offers a fantastic vantage point for views of the surrounding countryside. Looking like a white ribbon laid on a bright green skirt, it seems to stretch to the horizon, when seen from the castle gates. The very first time we saw it, jet-lagged as we were from our flight, we couldn't resist going down it, right up to the Copper Horse, and then had to drag ourselves back two miles for a cab pickup at one of the motorways intersecting it. By the way, the Copper Horse is made of bronze and took so long to cast that George III died, and it was installed in the reign of George IV.

This time around we were just wandering around the park enjoying the great weather and watching a long line of cars in single file on The Long Walk inch their way to the gates. The cars disgorged their occupants at the gate, and the ceremoniously dressed flunkeys ran a thorough security check on them before grudgingly allowing them in. These guests were dressed to the nines, with the men in their penguin suits and the women in their rich jewel-toned gowns with brilliant jewellery. With pains they had taken, I do hope they got an excellent lunch with His Majesty! It's astonishing that Packky feels not the least desire to see the castle innards so that we haven't ever visited either Buckingham Palace or Windsor Castle! As far as I'm concerned, paying thirty pounds to gawp at someone else's wealth is unfathomable! And so I happily spent ten pounds—out of the sixty I saved notionally—on guzzling some excellent ale at The Two Brewers' pub, a historic one at the gates of the Park.

There was a lot of maintenance work going on around the castle, this time around, and walking back to the main shopping street,

Peascod Street, was like going through a minefield! Just at the corner of this street, in the shadow of the castle, used to be a small shop selling lavender products, called poetically, the Woods of Windsor! This small apothecary served not only Windsor but also the Royal Family and had the Queen's stamp of approval! In 2010, Packky and her sister bought almost every product they had on their shelves, and presumably that's why they closed up the shop forever, causing great grief in certain quarters. I think, however, that if I hunt carefully in my cupboards, I could still unearth some bottles of the sweet-smelling lotion with the tiny purple flowers on their labels. With that danger averted by providence, we strolled down Peascod Street, nodding along to the golden oldies being belted out by a tall, thin black singer with a powerful voice, accompanying himself on the guitar. Spotting a Starbucks here, we stopped to buy the only thing that Packky buys here – a pumpkin spice frappe. Trying it gingerly for the first time, I decided it was quite nice, though a tad too sweet, and after buying some lavender soap, bid goodbye to the Woods of Windsor.

15

Epilogue

Ti, though otherwise a kind hostess, was a stickler for some things. One of which was her check-in and check-out times. Our flight from Heathrow was in the late afternoon, and we would have appreciated an extra hour or two in our cosy suite. Especially as we had to pack and stuff three weeks of wandering and collecting, well, stuff, into our bags, making sure that power banks didn't go into check-in or liquids into hand baggage. New and expensive items were carried in hand baggage, and any of Ti's items that decided to take a trip to India were kindly but firmly denied a visa. Knowing her obsession with her electric kettle and teacups, I washed up after my last cuppa, holding the cups as if they were Ti's heart during cardiac surgery and giving the kettle a loving wipe down, to have it pristine for her.

At precisely 10 a.m., Ti rang our bell, and we were ready to depart. She was fulsome with her compliments and warm in her entreaties to visit London again. Not to be outdone, Packky told her how we'd enjoyed our little sojourn and that she must visit India soon! The two ladies were happily chatting away, and I picked up both the suitcases and descended the first step, only to hear both of them admonish me in one voice not to carry both the bags down together. But I'd been strength training for two years and besides had watched Ti handle our big suitcase when we arrived as if it was a toy! So, I confidently and at a smart pace descended two floors! Alas! I was fated to come a cropper, as I missed the last three steps, while I turned my ankle and landed flat on my back on the first-floor landing, with my suitcases lying at odd angles, just like my foot. The two women carrying the rest of the luggage came scolding and tut-tutting down! I saw fear on Ti's face, wondering whether she'd have a long-term houseguest with a broken ankle. To my further agony, she hefted the bags upright and then did the same for me. I tried to gingerly rest some weight on my foot, and though it was very painful, I could do it. I was not going to let even a possibly broken ankle stand between me and my beloved home, and I think Ti was secretly but devoutly thankful for it.

By now, our Uber driver was impatient to whisk us to Heathrow. After stowing our luggage in the boot, Packky hugged Ti, and in thankfulness that we were really off, Ti turned and gave me a tight hug too. At Heathrow, Packky managed manfully to wrestle our bags onto a trolley and solicitously asked me if I wanted a wheelchair.

Pooh-poohing that notion, I limped through all the formalities, occasionally wincing when a particularly bad twinge snaked through the ankle, and then sank thankfully into a plush sofa of the lounge. Here, I proceeded to anaesthetise myself with one of the only two legal drugs in the world, stuffing the ice, from the whisky glass, into the sock around my right ankle and pouring the golden liquid down my throat. That and a couple of painkillers kept me going until I reached Mumbai the next morning. However, when I took off my soggy sock, my ankle was swollen like a puff pastry, and with one look at it my friend, an orthopaedic surgeon, advised three weeks of rest and a raised ankle. Since my ankle was not broken, he diagnosed a ligament tear and strapped it in a neat figure of 8, admonishing me to stay put at home and not to put any weight on that ankle.

Having looked forward, greatly, to going back to work and meeting my colleagues, I wondered, forlornly, what I would do with myself for three weeks, as the wife went trotting off to her nursing home. Then it was, that the kiss to the Blarney Stone, took hold of me, and I began to write furiously… Cruising *with* Packky!

Author's Bio

Dr. Shrinivas Ranade has worn various hats throughout his long career. Starting out as a family practitioner, he went on to become an 'Industrial Health & Hygiene' specialist and headed healthcare for Mahindra & Mahindra ltd., as their Chief Medical Officer, over the last eleven years. Crucially, he oversaw their entire healthcare, during the COVID pandemic, which made for challenging work. Through it all, he has written short articles on various topics, including medicine. He has a humorous take on everything around him, especially his wife – Packky.

Dr. Mugdha Ranade is an eye surgeon practising at her own nursing home in Mumbai. She has a passion for travelling that earned her the soubriquet "Packky" from her husband. She has combined her love for her profession, with as much extensive travel as possible. The English language, in all its various acrobatics and semantics, is a passion for her, and she has helped shape this book in more ways than obvious, not the least, by allowing her husband's unbridled sense of humour.

Illustrations in the book by Bhushan Udgirkar.

www.ingramcontent.com/pod-product-compliance
Lightning Source LLC
LaVergne TN
LVHW091054150826
845673LV00002B/579

* 9 7 9 8 8 9 6 3 2 3 0 7 5 *